SCOTTISH HIGHER HI

BRITAIN and SCOTLAND

1850s–1979

John A. Kerr

Hodder Gibson

A MEMBER OF THE HODDER HEADLINE GROUP

Dedication

For Marina – 'life beyond work'.

The Publishers would like to thank the following for permission to reproduce copyright material:

Photo credits

© Trustees British Museum, London (page 2); TopFoto (pages 4, 29, 37 left, 58, 79, 90); TopFoto/Museum of London/HIP (pages 5, 24, 54, 55); The National Archives, Kew (pages 6, 43, 63, 92, 94); TopFoto/HIP (page 7); Getty Images/Hulton Archive (pages 14, 46, 81, 131); Empics/Kirsty Wigglesworth (page 16); Courtesy Monster Raving Looney Party (page 17); Museum of London (pages 20, 22, 28 bottom); Bridgeman Art Library Peace Concluded, 1856 by Millais, Sir John Everett (1829–96) Minneapolis Institute of Arts, MI, USA (page 21); Glasgow City Archives (pages 23, 31); Orkney Archives (page 26); Museum of Edinburgh (pages 27 top, 114 bottom, 121); Mary Evans Picture Library (pages 28, 41); Empics/PA (pages 33, 108 right); Roy Lambeth (page 35); © East Lothian Museum Service/licensed via www.scran.ac.uk (page 36); Courtesy Oxford Classics (pages 37 right, 53); Gallacher Memorial Library/Glasgow Caledonian University (pages 38, 40, 48, 50, 75); Corbis/Hulton Archive (pages 51, 88, 105); Peter Higginbotham/www.workhouses.org.uk (page 56); Topfoto/HIP/Borthwick Institute (page 57); Aldershot Military Museum (page 59); Punch (pages 60, 70); The Salvation Army International Heritage Centre (page 62); By permission of Llyfrgell Genedlaethol Cymru/The National Library of Wales (page 65); Corbis (page 73); Courtesy timmonet.co.uk (page 78); Lorna Ainger (page 82); TopFoto/PAL (page 84); Courtesy Archant Regional (page 85); By permission of Llyfrgell Genedlaethol Cymru/The National Library of Wales /Solo Syndication/Associated Newspapers (page 93); Getty Images/Edward G. Malindine/Hulton (page 89); Corbis/Bettmann (page 102); The Scotsman Publications Limited (page 103); The Mitchell Library, Glasgow (page 104); ©DC Thomson (pages 106, 120, 127); Glasgow University Archives (page 107); www.undiscoveredscotland.co.uk (109); Rex Features/Roger Bamber (page 110 top); Getty Images/Christopher Furlong (page 110 bottom); The Scotsman Publications Limited (pages 113, 129, 130); John Kerr (page 114 top); Snspix.com (page 117); Courtesy People's Palace, Glasgow (page 125); Courtesy Marine Hotel (page 128).
Saltire running head © Icon Digital Featurepix/Alamy

Acknowledgements

Every effort has been made to trace all copyright holders, but if any have been inadvertently overlooked the Publishers will be pleased to make the necessary arrangements at the first opportunity. Please note that the publisher cannot guarantee either the authenticity or accuracy of source material and quotes within this book.

Although every effort has been made to ensure that website addresses are correct at time of going to press, Hodder Gibson cannot be held responsible for the content of any website mentioned in this book. It is sometimes possible to find a relocated web page by typing in the address of the home page for a website in the URL window of your browser.

Orders: please contact Bookpoint Ltd, 130 Milton Park, Abingdon, Oxon OX14 4SB. Telephone: (44) 01235 827720. Fax: (44) 01235 400454. Lines are open from 9.00–5.00, Monday to Saturday, with a 24-hour message answering service. Visit our website at www.hoddereducation.co.uk. Hodder Gibson can be contacted direct on: Tel: 0141 848 1609; Fax: 0141 889 6315; email: hoddergibson@hodder.co.uk

Cover photo © Colin McPherson/Licensed via www.scran.ac.uk
Typeset in 11/14pt Sabon by Pantek Arts, Madistone, Kent
Printed and bound in Italy

A catalogue record for this title is available from the British Library

ISBN: 978 0 340 888001

Contents

Contents

Introduction

Who this book is for

It is for anyone taking Higher History and in particular the Later Modern period, which is the option studied by the vast majority of students.

Why was this book written?

It was written to provide a textbook for students who are aiming not just to pass their exam but to pass well. Many other books are either difficult to read and contain too much content, only provide basic information in pass notes style, or are not written specifically for the Scottish Higher History course. This is the first full and accessible text book for the Higher History course.

What is in this book?

It covers all you need to know about the compulsory section on Britain in the Later Modern option of your Higher History course. All of the syllabus is covered so you can be sure all your needs will be met.

Why are there various activities at the end of each chapter?

Research in learning proves that if you just read as a means of learning, after 24 hours you will only have retained about 10% of the new information. Unless learning is reinforced it does not become anchored in either your short-term or long-term memory.

If, after reading, you attempt an activity which requires you to use the information you have read and process it in a different way than it was presented in this book then your memory will retain over 60% of your reading. That is why each chapter has an activity, the intention of which is to provide effective learning techniques to help acquire and reinforce knowledge. These activities can be applied to any topic with some slight adjustments. Some of the earlier activities in particular try to establish good essay writing skills.

Each chapter also ends with typical exam essay questions which will give you an idea of some of the ways the topic can be approached.

How to write a good essay

In the Higher History course, the unit on Britain between the 1850s and 1979 is always assessed by asking you to write an essay. That is true in the NABs, the exam and even the extended essay. It is therefore well worth finding out how to write a good essay.

Any essay you write must have a beginning, a middle and an end.

The beginning is your introduction. This is where your essay takes life – or starts to struggle; it's where you must do the hardest thinking, if not, your essay will probably decline into storytelling – gaining at best a C award.

Your introduction must:

- make clear that you understand what the question is asking you to do.
- make a brief reference to the title and state the decision or opinion you intend to support.
- signpost the main ideas or arguments you will develop or explain in the middle section of the essay.

TIP: *Revise for assessments by planning and writing brief introductions (about seven lines) to essay questions. Word-process them so that you can return to them later to alter or refine them. The exact wording of the question you prepare might not come up in an exam, but since the topic is likely the ideas will remain useable.*

The middle part of an essay is the longest. Aim for:

- several paragraphs, and perhaps leave an empty line between each paragraph. Good clear layout makes an essay easier to read and less difficult to mark.
- a new paragraph for each new point or idea.
- a key sentence to start each new paragraph which outlines what the paragraph will be about.
- paragraphs which show off your knowledge about the subject. The detailed knowledge contained in the paragraph must be relevant to the key sentence.
- a short, one-sentence summary at the end of each paragraph which links to the main question and makes clear to a marker the link between what you have written and the main title.

TIP: *As you are writing ask yourself, 'Why am I writing this information?' If you can't make a clear link between your information and the title of the essay, it's unlikely a marker will be able to.*

Your conclusion:

- must sum up your ideas
- must answer the question
- must be relevant to the question
- must support the ideas you put in your introduction
- should prioritise your main ideas so that you make clear what you think the most important points were.

TIP: *It is perfectly acceptable, and often preferable, to reach a balanced point of view rather than completely support one point of view.*

1 Democracy and the British people

Introduction

Between 1850 and 1980 Britain underwent great social and political changes which resulted in it becoming more democratic.

The study of **how** Britain became more democratic is straightforward. It deals with the social and political changes which took place and what new laws were passed to make Britain more democratic.

The **why** is more complex. What were the motives for the changes in laws? Why should people who held political power be prepared to risk losing that power? Why was the right to vote (the *franchise*) extended to more people? Was it pressure from campaigners or did politicians see advantages for themselves or their party at a time of great social change? Changes in ideology, public and political attitudes and a developing economy are all ingredients in the recipe of explaining why change happened.

Why could Britain not be described as democratic in 1850?

In 1850 there were two political parties, called Conservatives (Tories) and Liberals (Whigs), but there was no such thing as clear party policy or ideology with which the voting public could identify. MPs were mainly interested in what they could get out of the system for themselves. Authority was in the hands of wealthy male landowners.

Although the Higher History course starts in the 1850s a first step, and a very important one, in changing the political system in Britain came with the 1832 Reform Act, often called the Great Reform Act.

Until that time little had changed for hundreds of years and although criticism of the unfairness and corruption within the system had been growing in the later 18th century, the outbreak of the French Revolution in 1789 turned the word reform into something to be feared and opposed by those in authority. They were concerned reform would lead to revolution and therefore was a threat to their lives and property. To understand that reaction you must be aware that the French Revolution led directly to the

murder of thousands of wealthy landowning aristocrats in France and even the execution of the King and Queen, and that there then followed 22 years of war with the French.

Changing attitudes to the franchise

At the beginning of the 19th century many of Britain's landowners believed that not only was change undesirable but also unnecessary. Such a view was expressed by Lord Braxfield during a trail of reform campaigners in Scotland in 1793.

> "
> *The British constitution is the best that ever was since the creation of the world, and it is not possible to make it better.*

But don't just assume that Braxfield and other members of the political establishment were selfish or that the political system was stupid or deliberately unfair. The growth of democracy in Britain has a lot to do with changing ideas and attitudes about who should have political power. Many students assume that those who supported the political system of the early- to mid-19th century were at best misguided, at worst simply wrong, but to do so is to forget that attitudes and ideas change over time. There were people who argued for reform but those who opposed reform also had a case. They believed that men who represented Britain represented the **land** of Britain. Therefore who better to do that than the landowners? For example, read what was said in 1829 about the political system in Britain.

Source 1.1

MPs are shown filling their pockets from a huge tub of money. This cartoon attacks the corruption that existed in parliament, with MPs benefiting from a system which left the poor powerless and thrown aside like so much rubbish.

> Britain is land. It is therefore the landowners – those who own the land of Britain – who deserve the right to govern. As long as the land lasts so does their commitment to sound government. The rabble? What right have they to vote? They own nothing of Britain and... cannot be trusted.
>
> *The Duke of Wellington, 1829.*

Today's MPs represent the **people** of Britain. Such an idea was alien to most politicians in 1850. In 1832 the mass of the people – the rabble as some called them – could be ignored by the government as long as they caused no problems.

How had the political system changed before 1850?

A first and very important step in starting to move Britain towards a more democratic system came with the Reform Act of 1832 – often called the Great Reform Act.

By 1832 Britain was changing. The growing economy was producing a wealthy middle class who resented being excluded from the political system. They asked why, since they produced the wealth of Britain, they should not have a say in its government. If they were ignored they could pose a threat. An alternative would be to absorb them into the process of government so that they would not challenge it.

Those who supported the Reform Bill of 1832 were not thinking about future progress towards democracy. Far from it! As you'll see, many politicians saw reform as a way of preventing greater changes later. As historian and MP Thomas MacAuley said in 1831:

> I oppose universal suffrage because I think it would produce a destructive revolution...we say it is by property and intelligence that the nation ought to be governed.

However he accepted that change was necessary, saying, 'I support this (reform) because I am sure it is our best security against revolution... we must admit those it is safe to admit.'

The point made about 'admitting those it is safe to admit' is important in explaining why change happened, since it summarises an attitude to parliamentary reform that continued throughout the rest of the 19th century and into the 20th century. The vote, and political responsibility, could be given to 'respectable' groups who would not want to change the system too much. But if they continued to be excluded they could be the focus of resentment, discontent and possibly, eventually, revolution.

What changed in 1832?

The reforms changed the areas represented by MPs to reflect the population changes caused by industrialisation. The right of some depopulated areas to elect an MP (or sometimes two!) was taken away and the busier industrial towns got a few more MPs to represent them. Middle-class men owning property of a certain value gained the vote but most people, including all women, had no political voice. Even after the reforms the power of the aristocracy in government continued and at elections bribery and intimidation still existed. Five out of six males still could not vote and the distribution of MPs took little notice of the population changes of the previous 100 years, especially the demographic consequences of urbanisation. The House of Lords could still stop any change it disapproved of. MPs were still unpaid and to be an MP you had to own property. Britain was nowhere near being democratic in 1850.

The Second Reform Act, 1867 – a 'Leap in the dark'?

In 1867 a Second Reform Act made changes such as the alteration of the voting qualifications, the reorganisation of the constituencies and the redistribution of which areas could elect MP. Those reforms took Britain further along the road towards democracy.

However, you are more likely to be asked to consider **why** political change happened rather than just list the details of reform acts. So why did a Conservative government pass a reform act in 1867 when it had opposed the Liberals' own reform act only a year before?

Historians see two main reasons. One explanation is the overall social and political climate of the time in which the Reform Act was passed. There were powerful forces in British society in the 1860s creating pressure for change, and as future Liberal Prime Minister Gladstone said in 1866, 'Time is on our side. The great social forces which move onwards in their might and majesty are on our side.'

Source 1 2

Gladstone of the Liberals (on the left) and Disraeli for the Conservatives were the significant politicians involved in the 1867 Reform Act.

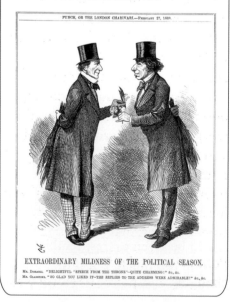

On the other hand the reform of 1867 also depended on the way politicians of the time exploited these forces for their own purposes. The Conservatives believed they would gain an advantage from passing the reforms.

'The great social forces'

The industrial revolution changed where people lived, how they worked and how they felt about their position in society. It was a major contributor to greater urbanisation, *demographic change* (where people lived around Britain), the emergence of class structures and the decline in the power of the landed aristocracy.

These social and economic changes created pressures which politicians in the later 19th century had to respond to. One of the biggest pressures was demographic change, particularly population distribution.

In the growing towns and cities the middle classes made their money and argued, quite reasonably, that since they were the wealth creators of the country they should have more of a say in the running of the country. Urbanisation also led to the rapid spread of ideas and the emergence of class identity.

The industrial revolution also demanded a more efficient transport system and the development of railways led to a national network of rapid and reliable communications. Railways, along with national newspapers, helped to create a national political identity and made the people in Britain aware of national issues. Newspaper owners saw the chance of widening their market and politicians were not slow to use the opportunity to spread their points of view far and wide. With the spread of basic education and the development of new printing technology, cheap, popular newspapers aimed at the working classes spread national and local news. In response, political parties organised themselves into national units with local associations, assisting the spread of national policies.

Political attitudes were also changing and political reform was

Source 1 3

Cities were growing fast and the new wealth creators wanted much more of a political voice in parliament.

no longer seen as a threat. The new political ideologies of *liberalism* (the right of individuals to express their opinions freely) and *democracy* (the right of adults to choose the governments which ruled them) were becoming popular. In the USA and in Europe struggles were taking place for liberty and a greater political say for 'the people'. Britain tended to support these moves elsewhere, so how could the British government block these ideas in Britain? By the 1860s skilled working men in cities (called *artisans*) were more educated and respectable. They attended night schools, took part in local politics and were concerned with improving their living standards. Indeed, during the American Civil War (1861–65) many in Britain thought of the conflict in simple terms of a struggle between the modern 'democratic' Northern states, who wanted to free black slaves, and the old-fashioned South which fought to retain slavery. Some British textile workers even chose to accept wage cuts rather than work with cotton picked by slaves in the USA as a sign of support for the North and to put some economic pressure on the South. Such actions and arguments convinced some politicians that the artisan class were respectable and responsible members of society having 'a moral conscience' who deserved the right to vote.

Pressure from the people

It is also claimed that politicians were pushed towards reform by pressure groups. It is true that groups such as the Reform Union and the Reform League, and demonstrations such as one of 100,000 people in Glasgow, certainly helped to persuade politicians of the need to consider reform. Historian Royden Harrison even combined the growing respectability of the artisans with fear of disturbances or revolution to explain why reform happened, when he wrote that the working classes had reached a point where 'it was safe to concede its enfranchisement and dangerous to withhold it.' He believed a revolutionary spirit existed in 1860s Britain created by a trade depression, which spread unemployment and a cholera epidemic which spread fear. He also argued that the Hyde Park riots of July 1866 and the Reform

Source 1.4

A poster for the Reform League.

League's campaigns all pressured parliament to make changes. However, later historians reject that idea, arguing that there is no evidence that parliament was forced to reform by external groups. In fact the Reform Act of 1867 created changes which went beyond what leaders of the reform groups wanted. So if social forces were only influential in persuading politicians of the need for reform, were more immediate, more practical reasons the real cause of reform?

In 1867 the Conservative Party became the government after 20 years out of power. Was the Reform Act therefore the result of cynical opportunism by the Conservatives trying to maintain their hold on power or was it a genuine attempt to spread democracy in Britain?

Political advantage

There were immediate political advantages to be gained from a reform act in 1867. What created the real chance of change was Palmerston's death in October 1865. As Liberal Prime Minister he had blocked any suggestions of reform for a long time, but after his death there was a new proposal for reform which split the Liberals between those who wanted reform and those who did not. This was the Conservatives' opportunity. They had

Source 1.5

As Britain seems to hide its face from possible danger Disraeli's face on the horse leaps bravely into the bushes marked 'reform'. Other politicians hang back, seemingly worried what reform might lead to. But was it really a risk?

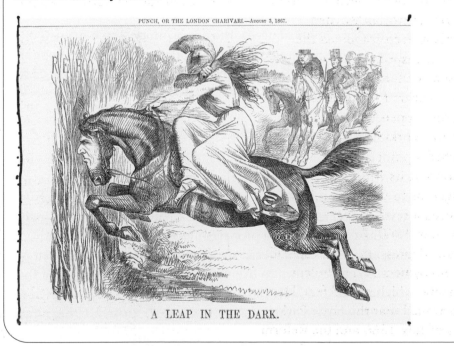

PUNCH, OR THE LONDON CHARIVARI—August 3, 1867.

A LEAP IN THE DARK.

been out of power for over 20 years and if the Conservatives continued to do nothing it was likely the Liberals would win the next election and the Conservatives would face more years out of power.

Historians refer to the Conservative Reform Act of 1867 as 'dishing the Whigs' by 'stealing the Liberal's clothes'. What does that mean? Quite simply, Benjamin Disraeli, the leader of the Conservative Party in the House of Commons, believed that if his party gave the vote to working-class men in the towns then these men were likely to vote Conservative in future! So in 1867 the Conservative Party stole many of the Liberals' ideas about political reform and spoiled their chances of winning support from working-class men. (An old-fashioned phrase for spoiling something is to 'dish it' and an old name for the Liberals was 'Whig'.)

This section has as part of its title 'Leap in the Dark' – a phrase used by Prime Minister Lord Derby when the Reform Act was passed. It means a risky move into an unknown area. But was the Reform Act really such a political risk?

By winning favour with the electorate the Conservatives were running no risk of really losing any power. Although the number of voters in boroughs (towns) was increased, the candidates they voted for were almost entirely members of the property-owning classes. The two parties they could vote for – Conservative and Liberal – also represented stability and old values, so the control of government was still in the hands of a wealthy elite. Traditional influences would continue to ensure control by the established social order so reform was no real threat to the system. Rather, it removed pressure from reformist pressure groups, responded to the social changes of the time and established the Conservative Party as a party of government.

Given their immediate political needs, the opportunity which opened up in 1867, and their possession of an outlook which allowed them to hope that Reform would be 'safe', one can understand why the Conservatives came to pass the Reform Act of 1867.

So what did the Reform Act of 1867 do?

It gave the vote to every male adult householder living in a borough constituency. At that time Britain was divided into borough and county constituencies. A constituency is an area of Britain in which the voters elect one MP and a borough constituency really meant a town or part of a city. By giving the vote to men owning property above a certain value and lodgers paying rent above £10 a year, the vote was extended to skilled working men who could afford to live in such property. The effect of this reform nationally was to double the number of men who were entitled to vote and in the growing towns the increase was even greater. For example, the number of voters in Glasgow increased from 18 000 to 47 000.

The Reform Act also made representation in parliament fairer. Boroughs which had become depopulated lost their right to send MPs to parliament, while growing towns gained the right to send more MPs to Parliament. Fifteen towns which had never had an MP now gained one while an extra MP was given to Liverpool, Manchester, Birmingham and Leeds. Some counties which had increased in size also gained an MP.

This redistribution of MPs attempted to make political representation fairer, an important part of a democracy. However the system was not yet fair, with land-owning interests in the south of England still over-represented in parliament while the growing towns were still comparatively under-represented.

The 1867 Reform Act was a move towards greater democracy. But as most men and all women still had no vote, and since voting was still open to bribery and intimidation, Britain remained a long way from democracy.

Activity ⫸

This section has identified two main reasons why the 1867 Reform Act was passed.

- Work with a partner.
- Leave a space for a title for this work.
- Divide a page of your work book into two columns.
- At the top of each column write a sub-heading making clear one of the two reasons for passing the act.
- Agree on no more than three sentences to summarise each of the reasons why the Reform Act was passed.
- Use light colours to differentiate the two reasons.
- Explain why it would be correct to say the 1867 Reform Act made Britain more democratic but wrong to say it made Britain fully democratic.
- Agree on a clear, short, memorable title for this activity and write it larger than the rest of your writing. Use a different colour to make your title stand out.

More Reforms – What happened between 1867 and 1885?

Between 1867 and 1885 more reforms took Britain further along the road towards democracy.

Apart from increasing the number of voters, reform also involved making elections and the process of voting fair and free from bribery and intimidation. Increasing democracy would also involve further redistribution of parliamentary seats to ensure MPs represented roughly equal numbers of people.

In considering the changes that took place at this time several approaches should be considered. First of all, what exactly happened? Secondly, why did these changes happen? And thirdly, you should be aware of differing interpretations about the effect and importance of the changes. For example, to what extent do historians agree with the opinion expressed by Derek Beales that, 'Between 1868 and 1885 the essential steps were being taken towards the democratisation of politics'?

Corruption and intimidation

Corruption was still a serious problem in British politics after the 1867 Reform Act. Despite increasing the electorate from 8% of adults to 28%, the newly-enfranchised men found their freedom restricted by the system of open voting and by the excessive spending activities of wealthy candidates at elections. Open voting required voters to announce their choice of candidate publicly and this clearly could lead to intimidation, threats and loss of homes and jobs if the voter did not support the choice of his employer. For example, in Bradford, England, voters working in woollen mills overwhelmingly supported the mill owner's preferred choice of candidate.

Greater fairness

The Secret Ballot Act of 1872 certainly helped remove the more obvious examples of intimidation and bribery but corruption continued. Candidates eager to 'buy' votes could offer food and drink and even jobs to likely voters. The spending on 'election expenses' rose to huge sums, but in 1883 the Corrupt and Illegal Practices Act limited how much candidates could spend during election time and banned such activities as the buying of food or drink for voters. A detailed definition of what illegal and corrupt election practices meant was created and all election expenses had to be accounted for. The law even stated how many carriages could be used by political parties carrying voters to vote.

Reform and redistribution

The power of the land-owning aristocracy of Britain was declining, but they had prevented the 1867 Act from going further and giving the vote to rural workers. The old rural elite resented the increasing power of the working classes and while the Liberals argued that people living in towns and in rural areas should have equal rights, the Conservatives resisted such ideas. However, in 1884 Prime Minister Gladstone proposed further parliamentary reform, which would give working-class men in the countryside the same voting rights as those living in the towns. As he said:

> *Is there any doubt that the people living in the countryside are capable citizens, qualified for the vote and able to make good use of their power as voters?*
>
> *Adapted from a speech by Gladstone, 1884.*

In effect the Reform Act of 1884 increased the electorate by 50%.

Another reform to redistribute the constituencies of Britain became law in 1885. It was called the Redistribution Act of 1885 and aimed to reflect more accurately the changing population pattern of Britain. It also attempted to make each MP represent roughly the same number of people. The new law also took away from 79 towns their right to elect an MP while another 36 towns with falling populations had the number of MPs representing them reduced to one each. On the other hand, growing towns were given the right to elect two MPs while even larger towns were divided into several constituencies.

Why did the changes happen?

A traditional argument is that the Third Reform Act was the result of popular pressure. WA Hayes wrote about 'the critical part played by popular opinion in making the Third Reform Act', but in reality such pressure was not significant.

It is true that before the 1832 and 1867 Reform Acts large-scale organised demonstrations in support of change united middle- and working-class reform supporters, but before the Third Reform Act, in 1884 there was little widespread popular pressure. Some pressure came from trade unions, the Reform League, the Reform Union and public demonstration – on 21 July 1884 a franchise demonstration procession took three hours to pass Parliament. However, this demonstration was not typical of the time and few thought it merited a description as 'intimidation Monday'. By the 1880s the political situation was very different from the 1830s and now reform campaigners used contacts within parliament and within political parties to pursue their cause. In short, popular pressure had little effect on governments who had their own motives for reform.

Political advantage

Parliamentary reform was the result of new legislation passed by parliament. In other words reform was not forced upon parliament but was granted by it. In can therefore be argued that political advantage was at the heart of much of the change.

The political party most associated with the reforms of the later 19th century was the Liberal Party, which was a mixture of reformist groups

and many who resented the power of the old land-owning aristocracy. For example, pressure for a secret ballot came from reformist John Bright within the cabinet. Bright (along with other Radical activists who wanted major social and political change in Britain) believed that the increased working-class electorate would use their 'political voice' to promote social reforms – but only if they were free from worry about their homes and jobs. In other words only if they could vote in secret, free from retaliation by their bosses or landlords who might not agree with their choice.

A later reform, the Corrupt and Illegal Practices Act of 1883, can also be seen as a pragmatic, practical move by the Liberals. By limiting the amount of spending on elections some Liberals believed the advantage held by wealthier Conservative opponents would be reduced.

It is therefore possible to argue that political reform was an action based on the hope that reform would give an advantage to the party in power. The alternative argument is that reform was purely the result of external pressure on parliament, forcing change against the government's will, or even an ideological conversion of politicians who, as if by magic, started to believe that democracy was just a 'good thing'.

A further point in favour of the argument that reform was driven by a search for advantage is that the big political reforms of the Liberal government of the 1880s could be considered a distraction from major overseas problems for the government. Also, by placing the reforms close to the next election, the Liberals hoped to gain advantage from grateful new voters in towns more fairly represented after the redistribution of seats.

The argument that democracy spread because of a significant change in ideas and attitudes is also questionable. The reasons for reform, both in the later 19th century and early 20th century, had much more to do with ideas of the respectability and competence of new voters, echoing the earlier views of MacAuley who spoke of admitting to the political process 'those whom it was safe to admit'.

One illustration of the argument that change was 'approved' by established politicians came in the 'Arlington Street compact' by which Gladstone, the Liberal leader and Prime Minister met with Salisbury, the Conservative leader, to 'do a deal' over the Third Reform Act. To soothe Conservative worries over his proposals for reform, Gladstone promised another reform to redistribute the constituencies of Britain. The effect of redistribution created many 'safe' Conservative parliamentary seats in the growing suburbs of cities. Reassured that Conservative strength would not be hurt by the Third Reform Act, Salisbury agreed to accept the Liberal proposal.

Overall, when considering political reform it is more realistic to see politicians moving their attitudes to accommodate changes which, in the long run, they suspected were unavoidable. At the same time they tried to ensure that their own party political interests would be protected in times of change. Clearly the political leaders of Britain trusted and controlled the reform process. Reform was not the result of pressure groups forcing change.

What really changed?

The practical effects of the reforms were obvious. The process of voting became peaceful and orderly. Whereas in some constituencies before 1872 over 400 police were needed to keep order, newspapers reported, 'Since the passing of the ballot act we have never had the slightest trouble at any election.'

However the more important question as to whether or not the reforms made Britain a much more democratic society remains unclear. Joseph Chamberlain called the Third Reform Act 'the greatest revolution this country has ever undergone' and foresaw 'government of the people by the people'. But was it?

If such an opinion was true, why then did later historians comment, 'the reforms were a dazzling display of change' covering up 'continuity of background attitudes'. As DG Wright wrote:

> "
> *By modern standards, Victorian democracy was undemocratic. Although the democratic principle was accepted in 1867, one man, one vote never existed in Victorian Britain, even after the Third Reform Act.*

The reforms of 1868–1885 had an immediate effect on the process of voting and representation in parliament but in terms of their impact on moving towards 'people power', little changed. But perhaps that was the intention. As was written at the time 'the grand object (of reform) is to appear to create a great many new voters, but really create no new influence.'

After the reforms, the system favoured a party with resources and the ability to efficiently organise those entitled to vote, while old traditional interests still influenced an electorate accustomed to 'acknowledging its betters'. In Blackburn one MP continued unchallenged for 24 years. Could it have been because of his party's donations to local football clubs, churches and other organisations?

Even voting was not made completely fair. One feature of 19th century voting (which remained into the 20th century) which seemed undemocratic was plural voting. Men who owned property in a constituency different from the one they lived in gained an extra vote (or more depending on the

Democracy and the British people

businesses they owned) while university graduates had a vote in their home constituency and their university one.

Were there other developments pushing Britain towards democracy?

To judge whether or not a state is democratic it is never enough to simply count the number of voters. In 1930s Germany or 1990s Iraq people had the right to vote, but these were not democracies. While the growth of democracy in Britain is usually charted by an examination of laws passed to extend or assist the franchise, also bear in mind the developments which provided foundations on which to build a democratic society.

For example, the development of elementary (or primary) education for all in the 1870s provided a literate society who could read the increasing number of newspapers, themselves a result not only of the increasingly literate and interested market but also of technology which allowed the efficient production and distribution of information. The growth of public libraries and the spread of the railways also provided greater access to information, and the railways also helped break down the insularity of Britain and the development of a national political consciousness. By the 1880s the British people were well informed about national political issues and were greedy to see the political celebrities of the day. Modern-day disillusion with politics had not set in and when Prime Minister Gladstone used the railways for tours around Midlothian, Scotland, 'thousands

Source 1.6

Gladstone used the rail network to travel all over south east Scotland during his campaign of the 1880s.

flocked from neighbouring towns and villages to hear Mr Gladstone speak. Where there were 6000 seats, there were 50,000 applications for seats'.

On the other hand, older, more traditional politicians complained, 'This dirty business of making political speeches is an aggravation we owe entirely to Mr Gladstone'. However the point was made. The public were informed and now saw themselves as part of the political process. The idea of democracy in Britain had become well rooted by the later 19th century but further change was still necessary. Electors had little choice, women had no right to vote and the power of the House of Lords was still unrestricted.

Perhaps Joseph Chamberlain was rather premature when he described political change at the end of the 19th century as, 'a revolution which has been peacefully and silently accomplished. The centre of power has been shifted.' Nevertheless, by 1900 Britain had become much more democratic than in it had been in 1850.

Greater democracy after 1900

After 1900, issues concerning the spread of democracy focused on three main areas. The first was restricting the power of the unelected House of Lords. The second was to allow the participation of all men in the entire political process, not just voting. Finally, there was the issue of votes for women.

Reforming the House of Lords

In 1900 the House of Lords was not elected yet it had power to veto, or block, any of the proposals for new laws or bills made by the elected House of Commons. The power of the unelected House of Lords was a direct contradiction to any suggestion that Britain was a democratic state.

Although proposals for reforming the Lords had been made in the later 19th century and again in the early 1900s nothing had come of them. The Lords had even blocked reform proposals to increase democracy, such as plans to abolish plural voting.

The catalyst for change came when the Liberal government wanted to pass a series of social reforms. These reforms would cost money, so the government planned to raise taxes by means of a Budget (officially called a Money Bill). The 1909 Budget was nicknamed The People's Budget in view of the social reforms, to be paid for partly by increased taxation.

However, before the taxes could be raised the budget would have to become law and that needed the approval of the House of Lords. The Conservatives, who had a large majority in the House of Lords, objected to this attempt to 'tax the rich to help the poor' and declared they intended to veto the budget.

1

The Liberals reacted by making speeches in working-class areas on behalf of their reforms and portraying the Lords as men who were using their privileged position to stop the poor from getting a better life. The result was that the House of Lords became extremely unpopular with the British people and the Liberal government decided to take action to reduce its powers. After a long argument and two more elections the Lords agreed to accept a Parliament Act in 1911 which drastically cut the powers of the Lords.

The Parliament Act of 1911 was an important step on the road to democracy in Britain. The Lords were no longer allowed to prevent the passage of 'money bills' (budgets) and the House of Lords also lost its power veto. After 1911 they could only delay legislation proposed by the House of Commons for two years. The Parliament Act also reduced the maximum length of time between general elections from seven years to five and provided payment for Members of Parliament.

Source 1.7

Until 1911 the House of Lords had a power of veto over the House of Commons. The unelected Lords could prevent any bill it disliked from becoming law.

Participation – the opportunity to become an MP

In a democracy, people who want to be involved in politics must be able to participate. For most of the 19th century MPs were not paid and had to own land. Although the property qualification to become an MP ended in the 1850s, working-class men, who had to work for their living for fairly low wages, could not afford to give up their day job to become politicians. For Britain to be a democracy the chance to become an MP would have to be opened to everyone. In 1911 MPs were paid, thereby allowing ordinary people to participate more fully in the political process.

Later reforms

To some extent the Labour government of 1945–1951 continued the work of slow democratisation. Two surviving undemocratic anomalies – plural votes and the university constituencies – were abolished by the Labour government in 1948 and in 1949 the two-year delaying power of the House of Lords was reduced to only one year.

Later reforms relevant to the issue of democracy of Britain included lowering the voting age for both men and women to 18 in 1969. But by 1979 devolution for Scotland and Wales was still in the future while the House of Lords still contained many hereditary peers, lords who held political power simply as a result of their birth.

In conclusion, Britain was much more democratic than it had been in 1850. The franchise had spread to men and women, the electoral process had been made fairer and reform was no longer seen as something to be feared. Indeed, many of the governments of the period saw political reform as a tool to increase party advantage. Nevertheless, society had changed, sometimes as a result of political reform and sometimes as its lever. Parliament could now be said to be much more fully representative of the British people, while the citizens of 1979 had very different expectations of their government compared to the people of 1850.

Source 1.8

An essential part of democracy is that voters have choice and political parties represent all types of opinion.

Activity ▐▐▐▶

1 To make what you have read more memorable, it is important that you use the information in an activity.

For this activity you must use the information about the growth of democracy to create a spoke diagram with the main themes around the main question and then organise the detailed information so it is linked to the main ideas. When it comes to writing the essay you will then have detailed information already organised and ready to develop your main ideas.

The diagram has been started for you. You can choose to include the extra information inside the single 'spin off' box as it is shown here, or draw another leg – leaving the box and linking to another development/ information box. The boxes you have still to develop are choice, access to information, accountability and the opportunity to become an MP.

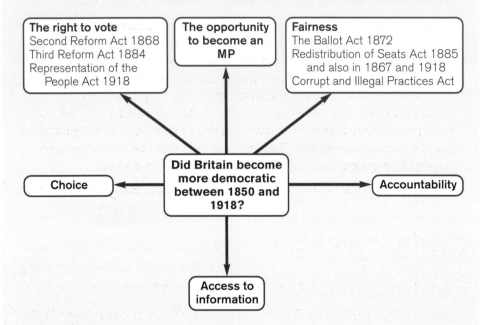

The right to vote
Second Reform Act 1868
Third Reform Act 1884
Representation of the
    People Act 1918

The opportunity to become an MP

Fairness
The Ballot Act 1872
Redistribution of Seats Act 1885
    and also in 1867 and 1918
Corrupt and Illegal Practices Act

Choice

Did Britain become more democratic between 1850 and 1918?

Accountability

Access to information

2 This activity shows you how to plan an essay based on the question:

Why was the right to vote given to more and more people between 1867 and 1918?

In the introduction which follows you'll see there are six numbered points. When you write your own introductions, it's a good idea to number your main ideas. This tells you how many separate middle-section paragraphs there should be.

Use this introduction with the following tasks.

There were many reasons why the franchise was extended to more and more people between 1867 and 1918. These reasons included (**1**) avoiding possible revolution, (**2**) trying to win advantages for a particular political party, (**3**) pressure from various groups, and the (**4**) effect of the Great War, which acted as a catalyst and speeded up change (this point is

fully developed in the next chapter). Another important reason for change was (**5**) the effect of the industrial revolution which changed where people lived, how they worked and how they felt about their position in society.

Finally, another important reason why the franchise was extended was (**6**) the change in political ideology which moved from believing the right to vote should only belong to people who owned the land of Britain to believing that the vote should be the right of all adult British citizens.

As part of your essay planning stage make six lists, each one numbered in sequence one to six. The numbers, of course, refer to the points made in your introduction. In each list find and write down as many relevant facts, names, events, ideas or quotes as you can. What you are doing is collecting information and organising it into the correct relevant sections.

Hint: The point about the Great War being a catalyst really refers to votes for women so read the appropriate section in the next chapter.

When you have finished this task the information you have selected and organised will be used to develop the main points outlined in your introduction. In other words, in the middle section of the essay you show off your knowledge – but in an organised and relevant way. When that is complete you will know you have developed all the points in the introduction and all that remains to do is write a conclusion in your final paragraph which answers the main question. Refer back to the tips at the start of this activity section. Your conclusion should be started with an appropriate phrase such as 'In conclusion …' or 'To sum up…'

Exam essays

1 To what extent was Britain a democracy by 1918?

2 To what extent did Britain become more democratic between the 1850s and 1928?

3 Do you agree that the franchise was extended as a result of popular protests and against the wishes of politicians?

Votes for women

Introduction

Although voices had been raised in the campaign for women's rights in earlier years, campaigning on a larger scale can be said to have begun with a petition from 1,499 women demanding that a proposal for votes for women be included in the 1867 Reform Bill. From then on the movement for women's *suffrage* (the right to vote) was a clear attempt to influence the development of democracy in Britain through pressure from groups outside parliament.

The failure of the English and Scottish Reform Acts of 1867 and 1868 to include women led to the formation of women's suffrage societies in London, Manchester and Edinburgh.

Source 2.1

Votes for women!

The campaigns for women's rights, and in particular women's suffrage must be seen within the context of a changing society and the huge social and political changes happening in Britain in the late 19th and early 20th centuries. A starting point to understand both the campaigns of women and the position of men is to look at attitudes about the sexes and how these changed over the almost 80 years between the 1850s and 1928 when women won the right to vote on the same basis as men.

Different spheres

A generally held view is that women in the later 19th century were considered to be 'second-class citizens', physically, mentally and morally inferior to men and therefore incapable of voting. However, a more appropriate description of mid-19th century attitudes towards women is that women were considered to be different from men, not only physically but also emotionally and mentally. It was argued that women and men operated in different 'spheres' with their social roles being based on their differing abilities. While men were the protectors of family and the 'breadwinners' who had a role to play in government and professional life, woman, by contrast, should focus on rearing the children and do 'good deeds' in charitable religious and educational work. As was said in a parliamentary debate in 1872, 'We regard women as something to admire, to love .... she is the silver lining which lights the cloud of man's existence.' A comment by Sarah Sewell, herself opposed to women's suffrage, is often used to represent the stereotype of wife and mother – 'The profoundly educated women rarely make good wives or mothers.' She continued that such educated women, 'seldom have much knowledge of pies and puddings... nor do they enjoy the interesting work of attending to small children.'

Source 2.2

This mid-19th century painting reflects an idealised vision of women as rearing children, helping their husbands and being fulfilled by their work in the home.

It was also argued that 'political' women would neglect their female duties and lose their femininity. Women were said to be too emotionally unstable for rational thought and, ruled by their hearts and bodies, were clearly unsuited to serious matters and fit only for 'women's work'. On top of these accusations of inferiority, Queen Victoria simply fed anti-feminist prejudices by describing the women's suffrage campaign as 'that mad wicked folly of women's rights.'

Under the law it also seems at first sight that women really were treated as second-class citizens. In the mid 19th century when a woman married and was 'given away' (by one man to another) all her possessions became her husband's, including clothes and any money she earned. Women had no legal rights over their children and husbands could legally imprison their wives and even beat them with a stick. Women who spoke out against this were told that they were already well represented in parliament, the courts and the world in general by their fathers, brothers and husbands. But change was happening and it would be wrong to assume that these descriptions of women as dependent, second-class citizens held true for all women up until 1918.

Changing society

Social change was an important factor in creating an atmosphere of acceptance in terms of women's suffrage. Millicent Fawcett, a leader of the NUWSS, had argued that wider social changes were vital factors in the winning of the right to vote. Her argument was supported in a parliamentary debate in 1912.

> **"**
>
> *[Arguments against giving women the vote] are both out of date and out of place. They might have been correct and proper two or three centuries ago... but not in the twentieth century, when women have for years, by common consent, taken an active part in public affairs, when they are members of town councils, boards of guardians and... are prominent members of political associations...*

As early as 1793, in *The Vindication of the Rights of Women*, Mary Wollstonecraft argued that women were deliberately moulded as superficial, rather silly creatures, maintained in a childlike dependency on men. It was not until several laws were passed between 1873 and 1893 that the social position of women improved. The Infant Custody Act gave mothers increased rights over their children, even to the extent of allowing some mothers custody of their children after conviction for adultery. The Married Women's Property Acts of 1882 and 1893 granted women full legal control of all property they had owned at marriage or that they had gained after marriage by their own earnings or through inheritance. The education of women also improved from universal primary education for boys and girls from the 1870s, to universities increasingly opening their doors to both men and women. Women also began to take 'white collar' office jobs as well as their more traditional jobs of teaching and nursing. Of course the 'marriage bar' still applied, which meant that many women had to leave their jobs when they married.

Source 2.3

Anti-suffragist cartoons like this one often showed campaigners for the vote as rather plain, masculine-looking spinsters, suggested that 'real' women did not need or want the vote.

Now Madam... will you go quietly or shall I have to use force?

Politically, the status of some women also changed with the Local Government Act of 1894, which granted women ratepayers and property occupiers the right to vote in local elections and also the opportunity to stand for election. Women also became involved in political activity, joining political parties, working as volunteers, organising social events, canvassing voters and making speeches. However as was pointed out by Harold Baker MP speaking in 1912:

> The exact numbers of women who were serving in public capacities [is very small]... on town councils there were only 24 women out of a total of 11,140 ... and on county councils there were only 4 women out of a total of 4,615.

Source 2.4

Attitudes were changing by the end of the 19th century. This cartoon challenges the male belief that women were free to make their own choices. The cartoon shows women bound and restricted by various difficulties.

THE HELPMEET—Equal Partner.

JOHN BULL CALLS UPON THE WOMEN OF THE COUNTRY TO HELP HIM TO WORK FOR THE WELFARE, HAPPINESS AND EDUCATION OF THE NATION.

[With apologies to "The Tribune."]

Nevertheless doors had been opened.

The overall effect of these developments was to erode male prejudices. Attitudes that were once widespread were, by the end of the century, changing. In effect, the stereotyped views of women outlined earlier were seen as old fashioned and outdated by many Edwardian men. Women, either by their competence at work, activities in local politics or in voluntary capacities such as church or charity activities, demonstrated that there was little truth in the fear that women's political interests would detract from their traditional role as wives and mothers. Change seemed inevitable and in the words of Martin Pugh, 'their participation in local government made women's exclusion from national elections increasingly untenable.'

Why did women want the vote?

Put simply, women wanted the vote as a lever to force greater change. They argued that parliament would never listen to their needs for greater reform in the home and at work until they had a means of making MPs and the government take notice. Lydia Becker expressed this viewpoint in *The Political Disabilities of Women* in 1872 when she wrote, 'the

Votes for women

Source 2.5

The rising tide of women's rights is too much for the anti-suffragists to keep pushing back.

THE NEW M^{RS} PARTINGTON (OF THE ANTI SUFFRAGE SOCIETY)
"SOMEHOW THE TIDE KEEPS RISING!"

sufferings and the wrongs of women will never be considered worthy of attention by the Legislature (parliament) until they are in possession of the suffrage, and not until they are politically on the same level as men, will their education and their welfare receive equal care from the Government.'

With the vote women would have a political voice and a tool to combat the legal, economic and social difficulties oppressing women's lives. As Emmeline Pankhurst said about the vote, 'first it is a symbol, secondly a safeguard, and thirdly an instrument.'

However, even among those women who did want reform, not all wanted the vote for the same reasons and there was disagreement over which women should be enfranchised. Whether the vote was demanded on the same terms as for men, for single women only, for married women who were property owners, for all women, or as part of universal or adult suffrage depended often on the status of the women campaigning. Were they upper-, middle- or working-class women, married or single? Their different experiences affected the method and aims of their campaigning.

The differing motives and different campaigning groups

For upper-class and most middle-class women, social success was marked by a good marriage and producing male heirs. To escape from this prison of conformity, women in this class saw the vote as a recognition of their own identity, a way of wining some freedom to fulfil themselves and to use their potential to benefit society and themselves.

Single middle-class women saw the vote as a means of opening up opportunities in a world where they might not 'make a good marriage' since by 1901 there was a 'surplus' of over 1 million women. As a result these lower middle-class unmarried women would have to fend for themselves. These single women therefore saw gaining the vote as a means of creating greater change, perhaps opening up professions and other 'suitable' employment.

Working-class women needed a political voice to be heard in a world which exploited them ruthlessly. Without it women had no hope of challenging conditions of work in factories, farming or in sweat shop industries which were unhealthy and dangerous. Their wages were very low and hardship, poverty, bad health and early death was almost inevitable. Although exceptions to the rule existed – for example, in Dundee women earned fair wages in the jute factories while their husbands sometimes took on the role of 'househusbands' – the fact remained that working-class women had to work and for most the alternative was starvation or the workhouse. And nowhere were women's wages equal to male wages.

In conclusion, whether rich or poor, many women across the social spectrum realised that only by winning the vote could they significantly improve their lives and status in society.

The role of the NUWSS

For pressure groups trying to bring about large-scale or political change, efficient, preferably nationally organised, campaigns are vital. In 1897 several local women's suffrage societies united to form the National Union of Women's Suffrage Societies under the leadership of Millicent Fawcett. The NUWSS believed in moderate, peaceful tactics to win the vote, mainly for middle-class property-owning women. Later the NUWSS was nicknamed the Suffragists, in contrast to the Suffragettes.

The campaigning strategy of 'peaceful persuasion' used by the NUWSS has led to a common misconception that the organisation was ineffective and ignored by the government and can therefore be dismissed as a significant campaigning group. Such is not the case. Although membership remained relatively low at about 6000 until around 1909, a persuasive campaign of meetings, pamphlets, petitions and parliamentary bills regularly introduced by friendly backbench MPs had created a situation where many, if not most, MPs had accepted the principle of women's suffrage. Outside parliament the NUWSS had some success in winning the support of some trade unions for the women's cause and when the NUWSS reached an agreement of mutual support with the new Labour Party, the Liberal government became alarmed that with greater support and organisation, the Labour Party could become a real threat to the Liberal's chance of election victory if no change in women's political status was made. The NUWSS also provided a home for women angered by the Suffragettes during their 'wild period' – so much so that NUWSS membership totalled 53,000 by 1914. These new recruits seemed to want to stay part of the movement, but not be associated with the violence linked with the Pankhursts and their followers.

Rather cynically, Martin Pugh described the move of women towards the NUWSS and away from the Suffragette excesses as, 'probably the one positive contribution of the Pankhursts to winning the vote.'

The WSPU – the Suffragettes

Emmeline Pankhurst had been a member of the Manchester branch of the NUWSS but in 1903, with the help of her two daughters Christabel and Sylvia , she formed the Women's Social and Political Union (WSPU).

The Pankhursts were frustrated by the lack of progress achieved by the NUWSS and it is true that in the early 1900s newspapers had lost interest in the issue of women's suffrage and seldom reported meetings. In response to such apparent indifference to the campaigns of the NUWSS the WSPU adopted the motto 'Deeds Not Words' and used campaign methods intended to breathe new life into the issue of women's suffrage.

The new strategy gained publicity in October 1905 when Sir Edward Grey, a minister in the British government, was heckled noisily. The two WSPU members involved were arrested after a struggle involving kicking and spitting. The women were sent to prison and the nation was shocked that women were prepared to use violence in an attempt to win the vote. Newspapers immediately took notice, the WSPU was nicknamed the Suffragettes and the organisation had achieved its first objective – publicity.

Source 2.6

This advert for a meeting in Kirkwall, Orkney in 1871 shows the effort and distance women were prepared to go to get their message across. The speaker came from Galloway in the south of Scotland.

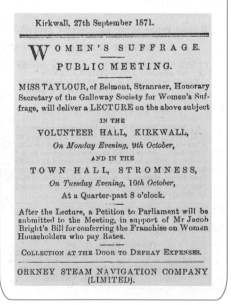

Kirkwall, 27th September 1871.

WOMEN'S SUFFRAGE.
PUBLIC MEETING.

MISS TAYLOUR, of Belmont, Stranraer, Honorary Secretary of the Galloway Society for Women's Suffrage, will deliver a LECTURE on the above subject

IN THE

VOLUNTEER HALL, KIRKWALL,
On Monday Evening, 9th October,

AND IN THE

TOWN HALL, STROMNESS,
On Tuesday Evening, 10th October,
At a Quarter-past 8 o'clock.

After the Lecture, a Petition to Parliament will be submitted to the Meeting, in support of Mr Jacob Bright's Bill for conferring the Franchise on Women Householders who pay Rates.

COLLECTION AT THE DOOR TO DEFRAY EXPENSES.

ORKNEY STEAM NAVIGATION COMPANY
(LIMITED).

Different strategies

When the Liberals won the 1906 general election many suffragists were convinced that the new government would give women the franchise. Indeed, the new Prime Minister, Henry Campbell-Bannerman, told a group of Suffragists that he was personally in favour of women having the vote – but added that his cabinet was opposed to the idea. When Campbell-Bannerman died in April 1908 he was replaced by Asquith, who was very much against the women's campaign. The NUWSS had already been pressuring the Liberals at by-elections by putting up their own male candidates against Liberals opposed to women's suffrage. When Asquith became Prime Minister the Suffragettes effectively declared war on the government.

Violent protest followed with a window-smashing campaign aimed against government buildings starting in 1908, and predictably the prisons filled with Suffragettes. In Scotland the most common form of militant attack was on pillar boxes, where acid was poured in to destroy letters. Further Suffragette violence followed in 1913 when suffragettes tried to burn down the houses of two members of the government who opposed votes for women, while cricket pavilions, racecourse stands and golf clubhouses were set on fire. Farington Hall in Dundee and Leuchars railway station were attacked and many public buildings – including Holyrood Palace – were closed for fear of attack, and security was tightened around others. Even old historic buildings such as Whitekirk Church in East Lothian were attacked if they were in the constituencies of leading politicians.

However, if the government had thought prison would starve the women of the oxygen of publicity they were wrong. Instead women prisoners used starvation as a political weapon by going on hunger strikes.

In July 1909, suffragette prisoner Marion Dunlop refused to eat. So began the campaign of hunger strikes, designed to embarrass the government if or when a suffragette died in custody, thereby providing martyrs for the cause. In Scotland force feeding was started in Perth prison where Dr Fergus Watson, who had

Source 2.7

At first both Suffragists and Suffragettes tried peaceful marches to publicise their cause, such as this one at Edinburgh in 1909.

Votes for women

already used the methods elsewhere, was an officer. Trapped between releasing the women or allowing them to die, the government began to force feed the prisoners but the methods used were frequently described as torture and serious health complications often arose as a result of force feeding. Watson was already responsible for the death of a suffragette in Perth from double pneumonia, the result of food getting into her lungs. To make matters worse, the women in Perth were held in solitary confinement. When news leaked out that attempts had been made to feed two women by the rectum there was a storm of protest.

Source 2.8

This photo from 1908 shows how Suffragettes used their release from prison for publicity.

Source 2.9

This drawing tries to show the horror of force feeding, which the suffragettes and others called torture.

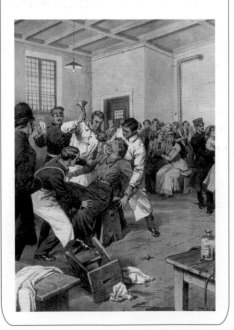

In response to the bad publicity generated by the force feeding of hunger strikers the government introduced the Prisoner's Temporary Discharge for Ill Health Act. Hunger strikers were left alone until they became ill, then they were released. Once the women had recovered, they were re-arrested, sent back to prison and left there until they completed their sentences. At least that was the theory, but released women did not await quietly the return of the police. Many women hid and police were bogged down in search and find missions. It seemed both sides were playing with the other, hence the nickname, the Cat and Mouse Act.

It is not true that the Suffragette campaign destroyed all support for the cause of women's suffrage.

Although support for the cause decreased it can be argued that were it not for the Suffragette campaign, the Liberal government would not even have discussed women's suffrage before World War One.

How important were the Suffragettes?

Books, newspaper articles, film and photographs have created a folk memory of police arrest, hunger strikers being force fed and even the creation of a martyr for the cause with the death of Emily Wilding Davison at the 1913 Derby. But were these events crucial to winning the vote? It can be easily argued that the campaigning of the Suffragettes brought the issue of votes for women to crisis point and made the issue into a political 'hot potato' that could not be ignored. But did the campaigns of the Suffragettes do more harm than good? As Lord Robert Cecil said in 1912:

> "
> *The cause of Women's Suffrage is not as strong in this House today as it was a year ago, and everybody knows the cause. Everyone knows that the reason is purely and simply that certain women have broken the law in a way we all deplore...*
>
> *The way in which certain types of women, easily recognised, have acted in the last year or two, especially in the last few weeks... has brought so much disgrace and discredit upon their sex.*

Even within the WSPU there was concern over the leadership style of Mrs Pankhurst. Unhappy with her domineering style and suggestions of greater militancy, 70 women left to form the Women's Freedom League in 1907. The WFL was not a meek organisation. It was prepared to break the law, for example, by refusing to pay taxes, but they did not support the WSPU's violent campaign of attacks on property. The result of the disagreement among women over the tactics urged by Mrs Pankhurst was that more and

Source 2.10

This Suffragette poster shows the workings of the Prisoner's Temporary Discharge for Ill-Health Act, known by the WSPU as the Cat and Mouse Act. The large cat represents the police and prison authorities. The 'mouse' is a small injured suffragette.

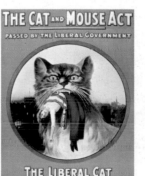

THE CAT AND MOUSE ACT
PASSED BY THE LIBERAL GOVERNMENT

THE LIBERAL CAT
ELECTORS VOTE AGAINST HIM!
KEEP THE LIBERAL OUT!

more women left the Suffragettes, so all that existed by 1914 was a small number of campaigners committed to the leadership of Mrs Pankhurst.

The actions of the Suffragettes had also mobilised opposing opinions, so much so that the anti-suffrage organisation founded in 1908 had evolved into the much more influential National League for Opposing Woman Suffrage by 1911. Given the diminished scale of the WSPU by 1914, Martin Pugh seems correct in his assertion that the enduring perception that votes for women were achieved by the Suffragettes is more the result of the Pankhurst's talent for self publicity, even when the organisation they led was losing support at an alarming rate, rather than an effective campaign.

By the summer of 1914 all the leaders of the WSPU were either in prison, unwell or living in hiding. Over 1000 suffragettes were in prison for destroying public property and public opinion had turned against the Suffragettes, so much so that by 1913 it was dangerous for any suffragette to speak out at public meetings. Anti-suffragist picture postcards and popular songs mocked the suffrage movement. By the eve of the First World War there were very few Suffragettes still actively campaigning.

A case can then be made that the Pankhurst's campaign of violence failed to shift the government. In fact their campaigns provided a good excuse for anti-suffrage campaigners to avoid the issue of fairness by focusing on the militant campaign, which seemed to provided an excellent example of why women could not be trusted with the vote. The tactical errors of Mrs Pankhurst also damaged the women's campaign. Her failure to ally with the Labour Party in a campaign to increase democracy in Britain ignored the thousands of working-class men who still had no voice, and Mrs Pankhurst was even willing to settle for granting the vote to some wealthy women rather than campaign for the vote for all adults. Mrs Pankhurst's policy both lost the Suffragettes political allies and gained the anger of working-class women.

Finally, when enfranchisement was actually being discussed during the First World War the Pankhursts had long since abandoned their campaign and had no influence over the discussion – only the possibility of a renewal of Suffragette activity after the war concerned the government.

In summary, the case of Mrs Pankhurst and the suffragettes shows that it is useful to remember that those who pioneer a cause are not necessarily responsible for its success.

The importance of the First World War

Britain declared war on Germany in August 1914 and two days later the NUWSS suspended its political campaigning for the vote. To encourage the Suffragettes to end their campaign the government released all WSPU

prisoners and in response the WSPU agreed to stop their campaign. With a grant of over £2000 from the government (which led to accusations of betrayal from the pacifist Women's Freedom League and more militant Suffragettes) a WSPU pro-war propaganda campaign encouraged men to join the armed forces and women to demand 'the right to serve' with slogans such as 'For Men Must Fight and Women Must Work'. The WSPU even changed the name of their newspaper from The Suffragette to Britannia. Mrs Pankhurst now wrapped herself in patriotism rather than feminism.

It is true that women's war work was important to Britain's eventual victory. As casualty rates increased on the battlefield and conscription was introduced to swell the ranks, women were needed to fill the gaps on the Home Front. Industries that had previously excluded women now welcomed them. Women worked as conductors on trams and buses, as typists and secretaries and nearly 200,000 women found work in government departments. Thousands worked on farms, at the docks and even in the police. The biggest increase in female employment was in the previously male-dominated engineering industry. Over 700,000 women were employed making munitions and facing considerable danger, not just from explosions but also from the chemicals they used. But has the importance of the Great War to the cause of women's suffrage been exaggerated? Did votes for women remain a 'live' issue during the war or did other factors move the government towards votes for women in 1918?

One traditional explanation for the granting of the vote to some women in 1918 has been that women's valuable work for the war effort radically changed male ideas about their role in society and that the granting of the vote in 1918 was almost a 'thank you' for their efforts. This, however, seems over simplistic, overlooking the pre-1914 changes of attitude and ignoring certain important points. After the war, for example, women were ejected from the 'men's work' jobs they had done during the war years and in both government policy and commercial advertising the idea that a woman's place was in the home was as strong as it had ever been. Also remember that the women who worked long hours and risked their lives in munitions factories were mostly single, and in their late teens or early 20s. The women who were given the vote were 'respectable' ladies, 30 or over, who were property owners or married to property owners.

Source 2.11

When war broke out the WSPU ceased their campaign and urged women to 'do their bit' for the war effort. This photo shows female staff at Bishopton Munitions Factory being trained by Glasgow Fire Brigade.

Another argument against the simple view that war work made recognition of women's rights inevitable is to consider the French situation. During the war French women worked just as hard supporting the war effort but after the war there was no 'thank you' in recognition of their efforts.

Perhaps, once again, the gaining of political advantage is a better explanation. The Russian Revolution had made governments across Europe worried about any social disorder. Rent protests in Clydeside (nicknamed Red Clydeside) had led to tanks and soldiers in the streets of Glasgow. Could the government risk a resumption of social disorder?

Such fears were not unrealistic, given that women who had done such valuable work during the war were, by 1918, facing redundancy or being pressured into returning to 'women's work'. Could the government be sure that these women would not join a revitalised Suffragette campaign after the war and return to Suffragette 'terrorism'?

Post-war changes

At the beginning of 1917, a plan to enfranchise women was being seriously discussed by MPs and a bill was introduced in March 1918 to give women the vote on the same terms as men. That idea was rejected but on 28th March 1917, the House of Commons voted by 341 to 62 that women over the age of 30 who were householders, the wives of householders, occupiers of property with an annual rent of £5 or graduates of British universities should have the vote.

Many MPs did believe that some reform was inevitable and that passing the female suffrage section of the 1918 Representation of the People Act would keep the suffragists happy and also delay more radical reform – such as full and equal voting rights for men and women. A general view was that such equality could be delayed by up to thirty years if the 1918 bill was passed with a limited female suffrage section.

Finally, one must take account of the process by which enfranchisement actually occurred during 1914–1918. One argument is that the issue returned only because the politicians grew anxious to enfranchise more men, many of whom had lost their residency qualification for the right to vote as a result of moving home for war service. Before 1918 voters had to be established in a permanent address for one year. It was politically unacceptable to tell those ex-soldiers they had that they had lost their right to vote, so the rules had to change. It was this that led to the review of parliamentary reform in 1917, in which women were included as an 'extra'.

Linked to that point is the realisation that the relationship between male citizens of the UK and their government had also changed. In 1916 conscription was introduced for the first time in Britain. Men were ordered to join the armed forces or do work of national importance. Was it right that the government could order men to fight and kill on its behalf and not

allow these men a chance to choose the government? That's why when the election was finally held in 1919 all men who had been in the armed forces were allowed to vote at 19 – not wait until 21.

The creation of a wartime coalition also opened the door to change. Prime Minister Asquith, an opponent of women's suffrage, was replaced by the more pragmatic David Lloyd George. His support for the enfranchisement of some women undoubtedly made change easier to accomplish. But those arguments may reveal too negative an attitude towards the women's campaign and their wartime efforts. Undoubtedly the sight of women 'doing their bit' for the war effort gained them respect and balanced the negative publicity of the earlier Suffragette campaign. It is even true that the actions of women during the war converted earlier opponents, including Asquith.

The 1918 Representation of the People Act also gave all men over the age of 21 the right to vote (and aged 19 if they had been on active service in the armed forces). The electorate increased to about 21 million of which 8.4 million were women – about 40% of the total number of voters.

Success at last?

At the time the 1918 Representation of the People Act seemed a major victory for the suffragist movements. However, there were women who still saw the act as a betrayal as it still classed them as second-class citizens to men. Politically, women were still not the equals of men in Britain who could now vote on an age qualification alone and also nine years before women who still had to 'qualify'. Even then, about 22% of women 30 years of age and above were denied the right to vote as they were not property owners. These women were usually working class although the new young middle-class 'flapper' tasting independence away from parents in rented accommodation also had no vote.

However, the politicians were happy. The NUWSS and WSPU disbanded and although a new organisation called the National Union of Societies for Equal Citizenship was established to campaign for the same voting rights as men, equal pay, fairer divorce laws and an end to discrimination against women in the professions, it posed no threat of civil disorder to the government.

Ten years later there was little opposition to the extension of the franchise to all women on the same

Source 2.12

Not only did women over 30 get the right to vote in 1918. They could also become MPs. The photo shows Nancy Astor, the first woman to take a seat in Parliament as MP for Plymouth Sutton.

terms as men. The heat had gone out of the issue and there seemed no reason to object to the further reform.

By 1928 most of the original campaigners for women's suffrage were dead. All except Millicent Fawcett. She was in parliament to see the 1928 Representation of the People Act passed and wrote in her diary, 'It is almost exactly 61 years ago since I heard John Stuart Mill introduce his suffrage amendment to the Reform Bill on May 20th, 1867. So I have had extraordinary good luck in having seen the struggle from the beginning.'

Activity

Your target is to teach a lesson, in groups of three or four, to the rest of your class which is linked to the issue of votes for women. Your main resource for information is this textbook but you must also research, find, beg or borrow other resources to make your lesson come alive. Think of the times you have been bored just listening to someone talk. Your lesson must be different!

- Negotiate with your teacher over how long you have to prepare this lesson.
- Your lesson should be presented in an organised, interesting, mature and informative way.
- Planning is vital – and all in your group must participate. It would be helpful to assign roles such as a gopher to go get things, a timekeeper to watch how your time is being used, a facilitator to keep things running smoothly in your group (tact and diplomacy needed here!) and a recorder to note ideas and what was suggested before you all forget.
- Your lesson should last between 5 and 10 minutes.
- It must have visual material – PowerPoint or OHP are possibilities.

As in any lesson there are really important things for you to decide and aim for:

- what do you want your students to be able to do and know at the end of your lesson?
- how will you asses the success of your lesson – in other words what will you expect to see or hear your students doing to prove your lesson has been successful?

Exam essays

Other essay types in this section could be:

1 How important were the Suffragettes in the campaign for votes for women?

2 Why were some women given the right to vote in 1918?

3 The growth of the Labour movement from the 1890s until 1922

What was the Labour movement?

The Labour movement was made up of two main parts. One part was made up of organisations which tried to look after and improve the living and working conditions of the working classes. Examples of these organisations were trades unions and self-help groups such as the Co-operative movement.

The other was the Labour Party which grew out of the Labour movement in an attempt to provide a voice in parliament for the working classes. Between the 1890s and the early 1920s trade unions and the new Labour Party used the power they had to influence the government of Britain.

Source 3.1

This union banner of the National Union of Mineworkers declares 'united you have a world to win.' The central flag states 'emancipate (free) your labour'. The appeal of freedom from the exploitation of the bosses was a common theme in the labour movement.

Trade unionism around 1850

Unions had tended to represent skilled workers often in craft or skill groupings, such as glaziers or boilermakers. The members of these unions guarded jealously their higher status compared to the unskilled members of the working class. These unions certainly could not be described as having revolutionary political aims. Most were concerned with the welfare of the members in the local area. They had few political ambitions. Nevertheless,

authority in the shape of the land-owning aristocracy or the middle classes saw any workers' movement as a threat to their profits, homes and prosperity.

In the 1830s and 40s the growth of large industrial towns, spreading slum housing and disease epidemics created an atmosphere ripe for violent outbursts – even revolution. Protest campaigns such as the Chartists made the middle and upper classes fearful of the threat which they saw growing among the working classes and particularly anything which looked like they were becoming organised in a united form.

Trade unions therefore suffered from laws at various times in the 19th and early 20th century which tried to restrict their power and influence.

Self-help organisations

In the 19th century there was no government-funded help for the poor or for those who became unemployed. At that time there was no welfare state. Trade unions tried to help their members as well as campaign for better wages and working conditions, while Friendly Societies and the Co-operative movement existed to improve the living conditions of the working classes and provide assistance to their members in times of hardship. Charitable 'friendly societies' had 4 million members in 1874 and provided benefits to workers who paid regular contributions. Working-class members were helping themselves to provide a better quality of life. For example, the Co-operative Women's Guild began in 1884 and within five years had 100 branches with 6000 members. It campaigned not only for the rights of women employees, but also for educational and political improvement.

Increasing respectability?

By the 1850s trade union organisation was becoming respectable. Victorian authorities were prepared to tolerate trade unions and socialist groups as long as the basic economic structure (which socialists called exploitation of the masses) remained untouched. The leaders of trade unions were prepared to negotiate and reach

Source 3.2

Friendly societies were self-help organisations, aiming to assist members in times of difficulty. These societies often had odd names and members identified strongly with the symbolism of their organisation, in this case a marching banner of the Pentland Shepherds.

agreement with employers wherever possible in an attempt to improve working conditions. But improvements were slow to achieve.

On the other hand, many ordinary workers in the Labour movement were not happy with a leadership so desperate to avoid conflict with 'the bosses'. Growing cities and large factories created the conditions for workers to share experiences and unite in militant action to fight what they saw as unfair action by employers. New union leaders such as Ben Tillett of the dockers or Will Thorne of the gas workers were emerging with socialist ideas which seemed to offer a brighter future for the working classes.

What was socialism?

Poverty, harsh working and living conditions and unemployment provided the conditions for socialism to take root. Socialists believed that the Industrial Revolution had made life better for the rich but worse for the poor. The ideology of Socialism grew as the extremes of wealth in Britain increased, and writers such as Karl Marx and Frederick Engels drew working-class attention to the apparent unfairness of capitalism. They argued that between the working class and the capitalists there was a conflict of interests called the class struggle. The capitalists were defined as the group in society which made profit for themselves by exploiting the efforts of the working classes. Landowners and factory owners were examples of the capitalists.

Sources 3.3 and 3.4

Karl Marx at the age of 64. His writings were a huge inspiration for British socialists.

Ben Tillett, a leading trade unionist and socialist described working as a London dock worker. In such conditions socialism could find supporters.

> " We are driven into a shed, iron-barred from end to end, outside of which a foreman or contractor walks up and down picking and choosing from a crowd of men, who, in their eagerness to obtain employment, trample each other under foot, and where like beasts they fight for the chances of a day's work.
>
> Ben Tillett, A Brief History of the Dockers Union (1910).

Marx and other socialists wanted the working classes to unite to carry out a revolution after which the profits which had previously gone into the pockets of capitalists would be shared among the workers. Clearly, those with economic and political power were scared of an ideology which preached the end of a system which benefited themselves.

'It is our turn now'

Unions continued to grow and in the 1880s new mass unionism really took off, with the formation of unions for gas workers, dockers and miners. By the 1890s there was a total of 1.5 million trade unionists, many of them militant and keen on effective direct action to improve working conditions and to raise wages.

Source 3.5

This socialist cartoon from 1909 illustrates the resentment of capitalist bosses who seemed to grow rich on the efforts of the working classes.

WORKERS—" If we don't get work we will starve.

CAPITALIST—" Some of you may have work, but my friend the landlord and myself will retain two-thirds of what you earn.

The new, younger leaders of these large unions represented workers who were prepared to fight for improvements in their lives. For example, in June 1888 young women workers at the Bryant and May match factory in east London began a strike and soon afterwards more strikes, including the dockers, added to the realisation that thousands of unskilled workers could form their own unions and gain victories for themselves. As a 25-year-old socialist, Victor Grayson said, in 1907:

> "
> *Through the centuries we have been the slaves of the capitalist class. Their children have been fed upon the fat of the land. Our children have been neglected. We must break the rule of the rich. The other classes have had their day. It is our turn now.*

The origins of the Labour Party

After the Third Reform Act in 1884 there was no national working-class party to attract the votes of the newly enfranchised working-class men. Instead, these men tended to vote for the Liberals and a pattern of working class support for the Liberals was established. Indeed, working-class men who were elected as MPs (often sponsored by their unions) were called Lib-Lab members.

In 1900 a Labour Representation Committee (LRC) was formed and soon became known as the Labour Party. It began life with two members from the Independent Labour Party, two from the Social Democratic Federation, one member of the Fabian Society and seven trade unionists. By the 1920s it had replaced the Liberals as one of the 'big two' political parties along with the Conservatives, and has remained so ever since.

The growth of the Labour Party was not as inevitable as some argue. In 1923 Sidney Webb, chairman of the party, spoke about the 'inevitable gradualness' of Labour's progress, but the extension of the franchise to more working men did not result in a rush to create a new party right away. The development of the Labour Party is more easily explained as a series of alliances between socialist groups, the realisation by unions that it would be useful to have a political voice in parliament, some helpful coincidences and the effect of the First World War.

Socialist groups involved in creating the new Labour Party

The socialist organisations of importance in the 1890s were the Social Democratic Federation, who wanted a genuine socialist revolution, the Fabian Society which was a small group of intellectuals and, more widely dispersed over the whole country and more sympathetic to trade unionism, the Independent Labour Party. Those three, together, were involved in the birth of the Labour Party.

The Social Democratic Federation

The most revolutionary and socialist of the groups within the labour movement was the Social Democratic Federation (SDF) led by HM Hyndman. By 1885 the SDF had over 700 members and was soon involved in organising demonstrations against low wages and unemployment.

Members of the SDF were unhappy about co-operating with other working-class organisations, believing that these groups were too ready to compromise their ideals in the search for votes or approval from the mainstream parties. Members of the SDF were believers in the socialist revolutionary ideas of Karl Marx, the 'founder' of communism. The SDF had little in common with the everyday needs of ordinary workers refusing, for example, to support the campaign for the eight-hour working day. They were dismissive not only of trade unions but also especially of the leaders of the older unions who were only too happy to reach agreement with the Liberals.

Unsurprisingly, the rest of the Labour movement were not very happy about working with the SDF. When the SDF argued that the new LRC should be openly socialist and become involved in a 'class war' their ideas were overwhelmingly rejected.

Source 3.6

The SDF was a socialist revolutionary group. This cartoon illustrates their desire to destroy capitalism which they believed was at the heart of all the problems.

In 1901, less than a year after the creation of the LRC, the SDF voted to resign from the committee, arguing that the LRC had no commitment to socialism and working-class interests. However, the SDF had isolated itself just as the Labour movement was growing in influence. By 1905 the SDF had split within itself and from the split grew the Socialist Party of Great Britain.

The Fabians

The Fabians opposed the idea of revolution and supported slower, gradual change through parliamentary reform. You could say that while the SDF supported **revolutionary** change, the Fabians supported **evolutionary** change. The Fabians rejected the ideas of Hyndman and the Social Democratic Federation and believed they should convince people of the truth in their beliefs by 'rational factual socialist argument' rather than the 'emotional speeches and the street brawls' of the SDF.

Nevertheless the Fabians, started in 1884, were a significant group on the road towards creating a separate political voice for the working classes and the contrast between the aims and campaign strategy of both the Fabians and the SDF illustrate the debate over the aims and tactics of the Labour movement which still exist today. Should there be a socialist party committed to revolution in the interests of the working classes or should a Labour Party aim at attracting support from many classes and areas of the country with the goal of improving the lives of people through gradual change?

Additionally, the Fabians did not want all power in the hands of the working classes. Although they argued that capitalism was unjust, wasteful and inefficient and should be replaced by a centrally planned socialist system, this would be organised and run by a specially trained educated elite who would move to a socialist society 'as painlessly and effectively as possible'. It was not exactly aiming at workers' control!

The Fabians were never a large organisation, having only 67 members by 1886. They saw their role as a fact-finding pressure group, issuing pamphlets on social issues and relying on other organisations to mobilise the working classes as a distinct political group.

The Independent Labour Party

In the 1880s working-class political representatives stood in parliamentary elections as Liberal-Labour candidates and after the 1885 General Election there were eleven of these Lib-Lab MPs. However, socialists and others within the Labour movement began to argue that the working classes needed their own independent political party. One such person was James Keir Hardie.

James Keir Hardie had been a coalminer and led the first ever strike of Lanarkshire miners in 1880. He soon became secretary of the Scottish Miners' Federation and gradually came to the conclusion that the working class needed its own political party. He founded the Scottish Parliamentary Labour Party in 1888, but he first entered Parliament in 1892 after having stood as the Independent Labour candidate for the West Ham South constituency in London's industrial East End.

Under the leadership of Keir Hardie, the Independent Labour Party was formed in 1893 and by 1895 the Independent Labour

Source 3.7

When Keir Hardie first went into parliament in 1892 he offended some people by wearing working men's clothes rather than the formal clothes worn by other MPs. Keir Hardie wanted to show what side of the 'class struggle' he was on.

Party had 35,000 members. But it still could not win decisive numbers of votes. In 1895 all ILP candidates in the General Election were defeated and Keir Hardie realised that, to win national success, the ILP would have to join with other groups within the Labour movement.

Although Keir Hardie urged the labour movement to unite in a campaign for genuine reforms to help the working classes, he was mainly a pragmatist who aimed at practical reforms that would benefit working people. Keir Hardie was not a revolutionary and was prepared to work within a parliament containing MPs of all classes. As a result other parts of the Labour movement criticised him. Beatrice Webb, in a diary entry of January, 1895 said Keir Hardie impressed her very unfavourably. She believed, 'His only chance of leadership lies in the creation of an organisation "against the government"; he knows little and cares less for any constructive thought or action.'

Were trade unions important in the creation of the Labour Party?

The answer is a combination of at first no, then later yes.

It would be wrong to think that trades union leaders automatically supported socialism or even the creation of a separate political party for the working classes. The leaders of the big unions saw their role as a pressure group on the Liberal Party and socialist ideas were not just ignored but positively opposed. Even when a survey was carried out to find out which groups in society benefited most from representation in parliament the unions leaders did not change their views. It was discovered that 650,000 miners were represented by five MPs while a few hundred coal owners had twenty MPs, but still the union leaders supported the Liberals and opposed growing demands for independent Labour representation. However, the attitudes of union leaders changed towards the end of the 19th century as employers continued to resist union demands for improvements in working conditions.

In 1893 the strikebreaking Free Labour Association was formed. In the same year the Home Secretary, Asquith, had ordered the shooting down of miners in a strike. In 1896 the Engineering Employers' Association set up the Employers' Federation, with the purpose of breaking shop floor union organisation. Lockouts became common. Finally, in 1899 the principle of picketing was attacked by the Court of Appeal in the Lyons v Wilkins case. The result was that trades unions could be sued on grounds of conspiracy.

Faced with the possibility of further anti-union laws, the Trades Union Congress of 1900 agreed to support the creation of a Labour Representation Committee. Ben Tillett remembered the creation of the LRC:

> *I was present at the Trades Union Congress in 1899 when it instructed its Parliamentary Committee to invite the co-operation of all Socialistic, Co-operative, Trade Union, and other working-class organisations in a joint effort to establish an effective political organisation for the workers.*

More importantly, the unions agreed to finance the Labour Party with money from the subscriptions paid by union members. That money came to be called the 'political levy' and union members were free to 'contract out' if they did not want any of their subscriptions to go to the Labour Party. Few bothered to do that.

The LRC was intended to promote the interests of the Labour movement in parliament. As Friedrich Engels put it, 'The first great step is to constitute (make) a distinct Labour Party... The masses need a movement of their own.'

The importance of Taff Vale

At first there was little enthusiasm for the LRC from ordinary workers, nor did unions rush to *affiliate* (or link themselves) with the LRC. Ironically, it was a serious threat to the existence of unions which helped the LRC to blossom. The event was the Taff Vale decision of 1901. The Taff Vale decision was crucially important not only to the development of the Labour Party but also to the very survival of the young LRC.

In 1901 a strike on the Taff Vale Railway led to the railway company claiming compensation from the union for loss of income during the strike. Eventually the railway company was awarded £23,000 in damages payable by the union but the longer-term consequences were a serious threat to the unions. If the Taff Vale decision was repeated, unions could be bankrupted every time they went on strike, denying them of one of their main weapons. In the aftermath of the Taff Vale case LRC membership rose rapidly since unions realised they needed a separate 'class' voice in parliament. The Liberal government seemed unwilling to help unions protect their funds so with more unions supporting the LRC, the income of the LRC income rose and it could now sponsor a number of parliamentary candidates.

Source 3.8

The Taff Vale strike was a vital catalyst in the birth of the Labour Party.

Why did the LRC do a deal with the Liberals?

Pragmatism (which means ignoring principles and doing what is necessary to win an advantage) was the real reason behind the agreement between the Liberals and the LRC.

With the founding of the LRC, the Liberals became concerned that in future elections candidates linked to the ILP or other groups within the LRC would 'split the Liberal vote' – in other words take away votes which would previously have been used to support the Liberals. While the socialist candidates would not win the election, the loss of votes from the Liberals might result in the Conservatives defeating Liberal candidates in many constituencies. On the other hand the socialist candidates were unlikely to win while so many older working-class voters would still vote Liberal out of habit.

The result of this dilemma was a very secret deal negotiated between the Liberals and the LRC. In a few strongly working-class areas, a Liberal candidate would step aside allowing for a clearer Conservative/LRC contest. In return the LRC would not 'split the vote' in other constituencies, thereby allowing a straight Liberal/Conservative struggle. Such a deal was very sensitive and could have offended people in both Liberal and Labour groups, so much so that the arrangement only became public knowledge in the 1950s.

At the time, the private arrangement worked well for both Liberals and Labour, as the LRC became known. In the 1906 general election the Liberals won with a large majority, but 54 candidates who were linked to the LRC in some way also became MPs. In the same year, the new Liberal government passed a Trade Disputes Act, perhaps as an acknowledgement of the help they had received from the agreement with Labour. The result of the new law was to cancel the effects of the Taff Vale decision and restore to the unions their immunity from prosecution after a strike. Trade union historian Henry Pelling wrote, 'the unions had secured from the ballot box the respect for their position which had been denied them in the courts.'

How did the Osborne Judgement of 1909 threaten the Labour movement?

Another decision by the House of Lords threatened the existence of the Labour Party. Remember at this time MPs were still not paid and Labour MPs relied on union payments.

The House of Lords (the most important court in England) ruled in support of a complaint by a member of a railway trade union called Mr WV Osborne. He objected to any union subscriptions being used to sponsor political candidates, and eventually the Lords ruled that since no provision for political activities or the political use of trade union funds had been made in any previous trade union law then union funds could not be used for political purposes. Suddenly the Labour Party faced financial ruin. In future anyone who wanted their union subscriptions to go to the Labour Party would have to take deliberate steps to make sure that happened (contract in). Most people would not bother.

The unions naturally argued that they should be legally entitled to spend their own funds in whatever way they wished. But for a time the Labour movement was seriously disadvantaged and the Osborne Judgement was not altered until 1913 although before that the Parliament Act had introduced payment for MPs, thereby easing the problems of the Labour Party MPs in Parliament who, unlike Conservative and Liberal MPs, had no private income.

How effective was the Labour Party before 1914?

Between 1906 and 1914 the impact of the Osborne Judgement and the Taff Vale decision were reduced, MPs were paid and several major social reforms of benefit to the old, young, sick and unemployed were enacted. The power of the House of Lords was restricted and working hours in shops, coal mines and sweat shops were reduced. But how far can the young Labour Party take credit for this? Did the existence of the Labour Party act as a catalyst for change, forcing the Liberals to take notice of this new challenger for working-class votes? In truth, the idea that the Labour Party was an influential factor in those changes cannot stand up to close examination. Although the Labour Party was happy to support the non-contributory old age pensions scheme started in 1908, the party was less keen on the social reforms of the Liberals which followed after 1908, especially national insurance and unemployment insurance. Both Labour members and the socialists had their own views on how to tackle such social problems.

By 1914 many people in the Labour movement felt badly let down by the Labour Party. Just before the Great War many in the Labour movement were disappointed at how little the Labour Party seemed to have achieved. Ben Tillett described the Labour MPs as 'unctuous weaklings' led by 'blind leaders' who have 'betrayed' the Labour movement. He continued by complaining that the Labour Party had 'utterly failed to impress' and that they had 'lost confidence in themselves and each other'.

Source 3.9

Ben Tillet, the socialist trade union leader, criticised the young Labour Party for not doing enough. But he did not have to face the reality of being a minority party needing to win votes in national elections.

However, Tillett was protesting from the comfortable position of not having to be elected by the public. Labour's leaders had to be realistic. They led a very small party struggling to maintain a presence in a parliament which mainly represented capitalist interests. To survive the Labour Party needed to attract votes from more than socialist union members.

The result was that the Labour Party had to be much more pragmatic in their search for votes than the hard-line socialists in the Labour movement wanted.

Essentially, Labour was divided by arguments over its commitment to socialism. While one section of the party argued that the capitalist system should be overthrown, the more moderate view, represented by people like Keir Hardie, accepted that parliament should contain all shades of opinion. In effect, the party continued to be divided between evolutionary principles of change and the more revolutionary position.

However, the Labour movement had been split in that way for a long time. Almost as soon as the LRC was formed in 1900, the SDF left the grouping to pursue their own socialist views. Some Labour supporters left the party to support Syndicalism which was a new, revolutionary idea to use unions as a way of attacking capitalism through strikes and more violent action. Syndicalists argued for a revolutionary take-over of industry which they would run in the interests of the workers.

On the eve of the Great War the future of the Labour Party was by no means guaranteed. Although the Labour Party had been making substantial gains at local elections and trade unions had been increasing their strength, the years immediately before the war was a time when the Labour Party had failed to make a big impact on the political scene. In fact the Liberals were attracting the most attention with their social reforms, conflict with the House of Lords and the issue of home rule for Ireland. In 1914 things did not look good for the Labour Party and observers thought that it was a matter of time before the young Labour Party was swallowed up by the Liberals.

Labour, Liberals and the First World War

One thing is clear, Liberal difficulties were an important factor in the rise of Labour, and those difficulties were directly linked to the First World War. In 1910, Labour's share of the votes cast was 7% yet in 1918 that share had risen to 22%. Over the same time the Liberal Party had split in two – one group supporting Lloyd George, the other supporting former Prime Minister Asquith. The result was that in 1918 the Liberal share of the vote fell from 44% in 1910 to 13.5% for the Lloyd George group and 12% for the 'Asquithians'.

Why had the Liberals split?

When the war broke out Prime Minister Asquith claimed it was 'business as usual' meaning that life in Britain could go on largely unchanged while the war was fought far away. However, Asquith's attempts to minimise the effect of the war on ordinary lives contrasted grimly with the mounting casualty figures and the need for Britain to reorganise production to cope with the demands of the war. In May 1915, Asquith was forced to make a coalition with the Conservatives and Labour leader Arthur Henderson was even given a place in the small War Cabinet.

Asquith was an 'older Liberal'. These 19th-century Liberals had always been against government interference in the lives of individual citizens but ever since the Liberal reforms a debate had been raging over how much of a direct role government should play in people's lives. The war was to cause that debate to explode inside the Liberal Party. Asquith's main opponent within the Liberals was David Lloyd George who argued that Britain was fighting 'total war' and extreme action was necessary. One such extreme measure was conscription. For the first time in Britain, young men were forced by the government to fight for their country.

The divisions within the Liberals finally led to Asquith being replaced as Prime Minister by Lloyd George in December 1916. This argument divided the Liberal Party into two almost equal halves and in the 1918 election the two parts of the Liberal Party fought each other and split the Liberal vote. The Labour Party benefited.

Source 3.10

This cartoon from August 8, 1914 sees capitalists profiting from a war that will cost the lives of millions. Disagreements over support for the war divided the Labour Party.

Death and the Profit-Ghouls.

(The workers of Europe are being slain in thousands, while devastation, famine, and pestilence overshadow their families, in a war entirely directed for the benefit of wealthy exploiters.)
Nobels' Shareholder—" Things are working out very nicely for us! "
Armaments' Firm Director—O joy and happiness untold! Providence is very, very kind to us."

Labour and the First World War

When the war broke out the Labour Party had also faced difficulties. Socialists were opposed to what they called a capitalist war and as a result the party chairman Ramsay MacDonald resigned and ILP MPs left parliament because of their refusal to support the war effort. On the other hand the Labour Party had gained respectability and experience of government by serving in the wartime coalition and when the Labour leader Arthur Henderson resigned from the coalition in August 1917 over the conduct of the war potential divisions within the party were healed. At the end of the war Labour was united but had benefited from the experience of wartime participation in the government before Henderson's resignation.

Peace

Internationally, socialism was on the march and Labour took inspiration from that. The 1917 Russian revolution had established the first socialist state and socialist risings were happening across Europe.

In 1918 it seemed as if Labour's time had come. Membership of unions had gone up during the war, more unions became affiliated to the Labour Party, Labour's finances improved and the image of the party improved as it campaigned actively for more social reform. The Labour movement had been divided by the war – some members were pacifists – but after the war a mood of unity took over.

A constitution had been created which meant for the first time all the various groups within the party accepted the same set of rules. The new constitution also made clear that Labour would be committed to socialist principles, as outlined in clause 4 of the new constitution. This section referred to an equal sharing of wealth and common ownership of the means of production. That meant that the government should, on behalf of the people, run the essential industries of the country. This is called nationalisation and became a main aim of the Labour Party. Socialists hoped that individual capitalists would no longer make vast personal profits while workers earned low wages. The profit motive would be replaced by a planned economy, planned for the benefit of the nation, not the capitalists.

Did the Reform Act of 1918 help Labour?

In 1918 a Fourth Reform Act gave right to vote to all men over 21 and women over 30. The electorate had increased from 28% of all adults to 74%.

Labour now expected to win many of the newly-enfranchised working-class male votes. But on the other hand, the new female voters would be unlikely to vote Labour since the new female franchise was limited to property owners or women married to property owners. Nevertheless, Labour did increase their share of the vote from 22% of vote in 1918 to 30.5% in 1923, winning 191 seats.

One study of election results in 1918 suggests that the number of seats won by Labour in 1918 had less to do with new voters supporting Labour than with the provision of more candidates to vote for. In 1918 the Labour Party put up 388 candidates compared to 56 in December 1910.

More importantly the Reform Act of 1918 changed one other rule to Labour's benefit. Until 1918 elections were still expensive times for candidates. Each constituency required a returning officer, almost like a referee, to supervise the election. That person's expenses were previously paid by the candidate in the election. After 1918 those expenses were no

The growth of the Labour movement from the 1890s until 1922

longer paid by parties so Labour could now afford to put more candidates forward for election.

Days of hope or realism?

The early 1920s were called 'Days Of Hope' for the Labour movement. There were high hopes for what a Labour government would do for working people when they got into power. But the problem was how to gain power?

Some historians have seen the result of the 1918 election as the start of an argument that still splits Labour – how socialist should the party be if it really wants to win an election? Did all those new voters for Labour really support socialism?

The identity of the movement was rooted in class identity but to win elections the party needed support from more than the working-class. To attract votes the socialist ideology of the movement would have to be played down.

Source 3.11

The title of this cartoon is ironic. In 1922 the Labour movement was still divided. In this socialist cartoon the Labour Party is condemned for its ineffectiveness in helping the unemployed.

1 Labour Party meets to consider drastic action regarding Unemployed problem

2 Adjourned meeting of Labour Party Conference to solve Unemployed problem

3 Further meeting of Labour Party Conference to solve Unemployed problem

4 Labour Party calls a Special Conference to solve Unemployed problem

5 Adjourned meeting of Special Labour Party Conference to solve Unemployed problem

6 Labour Party calls Extraordinary Conference to solve . . . .

The Labour Party Rescues the Unemployed

Meanwhile trades unions became much more militant. They had increased their membership during the war and in the early 1920s a 'Triple Alliance' between dockers, railway workers and coal miners raised fears of strike action that could bring the country to a halt.

The Labour movement was still split between those who wanted changes by strike action and those who wanted reform through parliament. In 1924 the first ever Labour government, led by Ramsay Macdonald disappointed many in the Labour movement.

MacDonald knew that the Labour government of 1924 was a minority, short term government dependent on the approval of the Liberals. Any real socialist legislation would have led to the defeat of the Labour Government. His ambition was not to make great leaps forward to socialism – he did not have the parliamentary support to do that – but to demonstrate that Labour was a reliable and respectable political option, independent of the Liberals. In short MacDonald wanted to show Britain that Labour could be trusted to govern.

He knew that to be electable the Labour Party would have to appeal to many sections of the population, not just socialist parts of the working class. On the other hand, socialists argued the Labour Party should appeal only to working-class interests.

By 1924 the Labour Party seemed trapped in the middle of conflicting interest. On one side the right-wing press claimed to have evidence to link Labour with Communism. Such a link scared off middle-class voters.

On the other side socialists were disappointed that Labour did not push through their manifesto of 1918 and claimed the party had lost its identity and sold out its ideology – in other words the party was not socialist enough.

The roots of issues which still divide the labour movement in the 21st century were well and truly laid down by the early 1920s.

Source 3.12

Ramsay MacDonald became the first Labour Prime Minister in 1923.

3

Activity ▐▐▐▶

Draw a spider diagram showing the main stages, developments and events in the Labour movement from the 1850s until the 1920s. There should be more attention to detail from the 1890s onwards.

- Give yourself plenty space. A basic, rough plan at an early stage would also be useful.

- Think about your use of colour in this diagram.

- One colour should be used to indicate developments within trade unionism and another colour for the Labour Party.

- How will you show developments which affected both groups?

- Different shades of the same colour should link connected points – for example organisations with the characters involved in them.

- Think also of how small cartoons or diagrams could make your diagram more memorable.

Exam essays 📄

Other essay types in this section could be:

1 Explain the reasons for the rise of the Labour Party by 1914.

2 Is it true to say that before 1914 the Labour Party needed the Labour movement but the movement did not need the party?

4 The Liberal reforms and the problem of poverty

Introduction

Between the 1850s and 1914 public and government attitudes towards poverty and how to assist the poor changed considerably. The laissez faire attitudes of the government declined as the realisation grew that poverty was often the result of circumstances beyond an individual's control. Local charitable organisations did their best to help individual cases but it was not until the Liberal government came to power in 1906 that nationally organised and state-funded help for the poorest sections of society was provided.

What were 19th Century attitudes to poverty?

In 1850 Samuel Smiles declared 'Self help is the root of all genuine growth'. By self help Smiles meant that an individual had the obligation to look after himself and his family through effort and determination. Smiles, and others in mid-Victorian Britain, believed poverty was a sign of personal weakness, either as a result of idleness or even genetic inheritance. Norman Pearson, a late-19th century voice on the topic of poverty believed that the poor were, 'seldom capable of reform' and that they tended to be 'made of inferior material ... and cannot be improved' He also argued that the poor were poor 'in their blood and their bones' and that they should be prevented from breeding!

It was as if the poor were being treated as criminals, their crime being poverty. The Scottish Poor House, or the Workhouse in England, existed to help the absolutely destitute, but these

Source 4.1

Samuel Smiles' book became the 'must read' book of the 19th century for the middle classes.

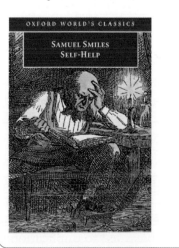

Source 4.2

Poverty was almost thought of as crime, for which the poor could be sent into a poor house.

places were feared and hated as institutions which signalled a person's failure and to enter such places was indeed shameful and to be avoided at all cost. As a result many of the poor depended on charity organisations.

Philanthropy (individuals doing good works to help the less fortunate) was a strong theme running through Victorian and Edwardian society. The wealthier sections of society felt it was their moral duty to help the poor, encouraged by a strong Christian belief that it was better to give than to receive. As a report of the Hackney Benevolent Pension Society put it:

> *To soothe the sorrows of the poor and to support the infirmities of the aged ... these are duties which are encouraged by the clearest dictates of our religion.*

Recent studies have questioned the effectiveness of these charitable organisations. Each organisation seemed to work in isolation, knowing nothing of the work of other groups outside their own immediate area. The lack of a 'big picture' to see who was being helped, where and by whom on a national basis led to duplication of effort, and as contemporary historian

Source 4.3

Extreme poverty haunted Britain in the 19th century, way beyond the ability of people to 'self help' their way out of poverty.

JR Green observed, there were 'hundreds of agencies at work over the same ground with no cooperation or the slightest information as to each other's exertions.' Partly in response to the fears that individuals could apply more than once for help to different organisations, the Charity Organisation Society (COS) was created in 1869. Their attitude was typical of later Victorian attitudes towards poverty.

> *The poor should meet all the ordinary contingencies (expenses) of life, relying not upon public and private charity, but upon their own industry (hard work) and thrift (savings). It is a hurtful misuse of money to spend on assisting the labouring classes to meet emergencies which they should have anticipated and provided for.*

This view was echoed by former Prime Minister WE Gladstone, who said in 1884:

> *There is a disposition to think... that the government ought to do everything... The spirit of self-reliance should be preserved in the minds of the masses of the people, in the minds of every member of that class.*

The Liberal reforms and the problem of poverty

Changing attitudes to poverty

In contrast to the beliefs of the COS, it was becoming increasingly clear that the poor could not deal with circumstances beyond their control. The assumption that poverty was in some way the fault of the individual was being questioned more and more.

A report from the Macclesfield Relief Association concluded:

> *How almost impossible is it, then, for a working man to be thrifty. He lives from hand-to-mouth... Directly sickness comes, or a few months of abnormally bad trade, there is nothing to fall back on; and what can our Relief Society do when there are several hundreds in similar plight?*

In 1889, the writer George Sims argued the case for government intervention.

> *There is a penalty for packing cattle too closely together: why should there be none for improperly housing men and women and children? The law says that no child shall grow up without reading, writing and arithmetic; but the law does nothing that children may have air, and light, and shelter.*

Source 4.4

Poor houses were unattractive places where the poor were kept as efficiently and as cheaply as possible. This poor house in Aberdeen used its chapel as a dining room.

While charitable organisations might temporarily help individuals, there was a recognition that such charities did little to reach long-term solutions and rather harshly, one writer described charity as doing nothing more, 'than manuring the ground in which these social weeds grow.' With rather more tact the Reverend LR Phelps of Oxford said in 1901:

> *Private philanthropy cannot provide a remedy for widespread want which results from broad and general social causes; it ought not be expected to do so; the provision of such remedies is the responsibility of the state and should be accepted as such.*

This statement alone illustrates the change in attitude towards social problems generally – an attitude which saw the solution lying with the government, or state, rather than the individual.

Why did attitudes change?

The reports of Booth and Rowntree

At the end of the 19th century, investigations revealed the true, and mainly unsuspected, levels of poverty in Britain. There were many investigations into living conditions but there were two investigations in particular which had a big impact on political thinking. These investigations proved that poverty had causes, often beyond the control of the poor themselves, which restricted the ability of men, and especially of women, children and the elderly, to control their lives. What could any individual do about low pay, unemployment, sickness and old age?

The first was organised and run by Charles Booth, a London businessman, who doubted the claims of socialists that a quarter of the population lived in extreme poverty. Booth decided to investigate poverty in the East End of the city. Working with a team of researchers mainly at weekends and evenings, Booth's work was based on hard, statistical facts, not opinion. In 1889 he published his shocking results as *Labour and Life of the People*. The book showed that 35% of London's population lived in extreme poverty, much worse than the socialists had claimed.

Booth then decided to research all of London and over the next 12 years, between 1891 and 1903, Booth published his findings in 17 volumes entitled *Life and Labour of the People of London*. Booth discovered the same levels of poverty throughout London. He then argued that poverty was such a big problem that only the government could really help and if nothing was done to improve the lives of the poor Britain was in danger of a socialist revolution.

The second influential investigation into poverty was carried out by Seebohm Rowntree in the city of York. Inspired by the work of Booth in London, Rowntree decided to find out if London's level of poverty only applied to that city or if similar levels of poverty existed across Britain.

Source 4.5

Seebohm Rowntree discovered extreme poverty in York.

After two years of research, in 1901 Rowntree published *Poverty, A Study of Town Life*, which showed that almost 30% of the York population lived in extreme poverty. People realised that if York, a relatively small, 'typical' English city had such problems then so would other British cities, and that the problem of poverty was therefore a national problem.

In his researches Rowntree defined poverty very carefully. He drew up a 'poverty line' which was the least amount a family could survive on. He also defined poverty as either 'primary' or 'secondary'. In the former, a family lacked sufficient earnings to buy even the minimum necessities. In the latter definition, poverty was the result of earning enough to stay above the poverty line, but then 'wasting' some money on items such as alcohol, gambling or smoking. However Rowntree recognised that such 'wasteful' spending might well be 'escapes', the need for which was caused by poverty itself. Rowntree also argued that poverty might not be constant, with families and individuals dropping below the poverty line at different stages in their life, especially old age.

The reports of Charles Booth and Seebohm Rowntree provided politicians with evidence to suggest that no matter how hard certain people tried, they could not lift themselves out of poverty. Poverty was shown by the reports to have causes, the cures for which were beyond the individual efforts of the poor. The concept of the 'deserving poor', those who were poor through no fault of their own, took root and was an important theme running through the Liberal Reforms.

Worries about national security

In 1899 Britain became involved in a war in South Africa, at the time part of the British Empire. Since Britain had a relatively small army, recruits were needed to swell the ranks. However, the government became alarmed when almost 25% of the volunteers were rejected because they were physically unfit to serve in the armed forces. This figure was even higher among volunteers from the industrial cities. Politicians and public alike began to ask if Britain could survive a war or protect its empire against a far stronger enemy than the South African Boers if the nation's 'fighting stock' of young men was so unhealthy.

Source 4.6

Charles Booth discovered that almost 30% of London's population was extremely poor.

As a direct result of these concerns an Interdepartmental Committee on Physical Deterioration was created to examine the problem of ill health in England and Wales while in Scotland a Royal Commission did the same task. Their reports in 1904 suggested that the physical condition of many adult males was poor and made recommendations about improving diet and reducing overcrowding. More specifically they recommended free school meals and medical examination for school children. Since these points were among the first reforms introduced by the Liberals after their election victory in 1906, it is clear that concern over national security had a direct influence on the reforms.

Concerns over national efficiency

By the end of the 19th century Britain was no longer the strongest industrial nation and was facing serious competition from new industrial nations such as Germany. It was believed that if the health and educational standards of Britain's workers got worse then Britain's position as a strong industrial power would be threatened.

There was also concern that in times of economic depression unemployment soared in certain areas while jobs existed in others. Politicians such as Winston Churchill voiced concern that part of the problem was that the unemployed did not know where the new jobs were. This, he argued, was an example of inefficiency weakening Britain's industrial output. A few years later the Liberals opened the first labour exchanges to minimise the time a worker was unemployed, thereby increasing the efficiency of the labour market.

Another development which may have influenced attitudes was that in Germany a system of welfare benefits and old age pensions had already been set up in the 1880s. Why could Britain not do likewise?

Source 4.7

This recruitment poster, used during the Boer War, hid the reality that many volunteers were too ill or unfit to serve in the army.

Political advantage and New Liberalism

Many historians believe that the Liberal reforms were not passed because of genuine concern about the poor but simply for political advantage.

Most working-class men had the vote since 1884 and the Liberals had tended to attract many of those votes. But by 1906 the newly formed Labour Party was competing for the same votes. So how justified is the claim that the Liberal reforms happened for the very selfish reason of retaining working-class votes?

Liberals had always argued that liberalism stood for individual freedom with the least possible involvement by the government in the lives of ordinary people. The 'Old Liberal' attitude was that poverty was due to personal defects of character. But as a realisation grew that poverty itself imposed restrictions on the choices available to an individual, a new definition of Liberalism grew up. New Liberals argued that state intervention was necessary to liberate people from social problems over which they had no control.

In truth the nature of Liberalism was changing long before the formation of the Labour Party in 1900. There were disagreements over the extent of reform but Liberal politicians were moving towards a reforming programme. There were, of course, a large number of Liberals who were wary about reform, and some who were willing to swallow their doubts because of the party's evident need to capture more working class votes – the party had, after all, been out of power since 1886.

By the end of the century, some Liberal-controlled local authorities had already become deeply involved in programmes of social welfare. Parks, schools, libraries, transport, water and gas supply and sewerage were built by local governments and paid for by local taxation.

Source 4.8

In this cartoon the values of Old Liberalism are being challenged by pressure from socialism. If the Liberals did not try to attract the newly enfranchised working men would they change their vote to the Labour Party?

FORCED FELLOWSHIP.

SUSPICIOUS-LOOKING PARTY. "ANY OBJECTION TO MY COMPANY, GUV'NOR? I'M AGOIN' YOUR WAY." —(aside) "AND FURTHER."

During the second half of the 19th century the public had also become used to increasing levels of government intervention in their lives. Nationally, a host of laws designed to ease the exploitation of the weakest in society and to improve working and living conditions, such as Factory Acts and Public Health Acts, had moved governments, of what ever party, towards greater intervention. In fact writers at the time wrote about the tendency of local authorities 'to provide everything the population required in its passage from the cradle to the grave', a phrase usually associated with the Labour governments reforms of 40 years later.

Nevertheless, New Liberal ideas were not important issues in the general election campaign of 1905. In fact the Liberals made no mention of social reforms in their party manifesto. When the Liberals took over the government in 1906 some reforms happened, mostly associated with the public concern over national security – but when 'Old Liberal' Prime Minister Campbell Bannerman died in 1908 the door was opened for new 'interventionist' ideas. New Prime Minister Asquith appointed 'New Liberals' such as David Lloyd George and Winston Churchill to top jobs, and suddenly a flood of social reforms happened. It was not a coincidence that the reforms the Liberals introduced or attempted to introduce after 1906 were a compromise between the varying views of the reforming elements of the 1890s.

The reforms dealing with children

School meals

By 1906 the issue of children too hungry or generally too weak to learn was well reported. A pamphlet written in 1885 by Annie Hicks declared:

> *It is impossible to educate insufficiently fed children without physical and mental injury. It is impossible for our working classes to ensure their children proper nourishment. I would ... support one good free meal a day...*

Twenty years later nothing had changed when the Committee on Physical Deterioration reported, 'It is the height of cruelty to subject half starved children to the process of education.'

In 1906 the Liberals won a landslide victory and became the government, but at the same time several Labour MPs were elected, one of whom was Fred Jowett, MP for Bradford. For some time Jowett and Margaret McMillan had been providing illegal school meals in Bradford, illegal in the sense they had no right to do so since the meals were paid for by local taxation. Jowett's maiden speech was on the subject of school meals, arguing that since the government had made education compulsory, then it

Source 4.9

These children are queuing for breakfasts provided by the Salvation Army. Hunger and poverty remain important influences in a child's ability to learn and grow.

must take responsibility for the proper nourishment of school children. The new Liberal government was convinced and in 1906 it passed the Provision of School Meals Act. Local authorities were permitted to raise money by increasing rates (a local tax based on property values) but the law did not force local authorities to provide school meals. By 1911 less than a third of all education authorities were using rates to support school meal provision and almost 30 years later still over half of all local authorities were not providing the service.

Clearly the Liberals had acknowledged the problem but had not forced through a solution.

Medical inspection

Building on concerns about the health of the nation exposed by the unfitness of army recruits, the 1906 Report of the Inter-Departmental Committee on Medical Inspection and Feeding of Children attending Public Elementary Schools stated that in cases where, 'The school medical officer inspected each child referred to him by teachers as suffering from defects likely to affect their education, e.g. defects of sight, uncleanliness, infectious disease, physical unfitness to attend, there have been specially beneficial results regarding eyesight and infectious disease.' However, the report continued, 'The local authority inspected but did not provide treatment; owing to poverty, a large percentage of cases went untreated.'

The Liberal government was well aware of the problems facing Britain in the future if the health of most of its children was not improved, so in

1907 medical inspections for children were made compulsory. At least three inspections were to happen during a child's school career, but as critics pointed out there was no provision for the treatment of illnesses or infections found, nor was there any attempt to improve the health of older children or adults. This was a very limited measure, the reason for which is revealed in the Inter-Departmental Committee quoted above. Their task was to report whether help 'to improve the health of children could be better organised, without any charge upon public funds.' Cost, rather than good health, was the prime concern.

Medical inspection did little to solve any problems so it was not until free medical treatment for school children began in 1912 that problems could be dealt with.

The Children's Charter

Victorian England was a dangerous place for children, who were often forced into hazardous work and abused or neglected at home. While cruelty to animals was an offence punishable by law, children had no such legal protection.

Children were accepted as the group least able to protect themselves from poverty and associated 'social evils'. Since many were born into poverty, they were believed to be victims of their circumstances and therefore judged to be 'deserving poor'.

Early attempts to protect children from 'social evils', such as smoking and alcohol, by setting minimum ages at which these things could be bought had limited success, while social reformers claimed poverty was a major factor in causing youth crime. The result was that in 1908 a Children's Act brought together the many rulings and decisions made in the past, all designed to protect children from neglect and abuse. The act ensured children were not living on the streets without food or education, and it also banned children under 16 from smoking, drinking alcohol or begging.

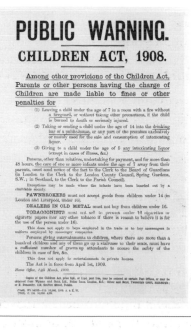

Source 4.10

The Children's Act was an attempt to provide a better start in life for children, partly by making it more difficult to get access to bad influences.

New juvenile courts were set up for children accused of committing crimes. Remand homes were opened for children who were awaiting trial to live in, rather than put them in adult prisons, and borstals were set up to deal with children convicted of breaking the law, to keep them away from adult criminals. When released from borstal, probation officers were employed to help and advise the former offenders in an attempt to avoid re-offending.

All these reforms were called collectively the 'Children's Charter' because it was believed this set of reforms would be like an old-fashioned document or charter which would guarantee better lives for children. The Charter contained many new pieces of legislation and some parts of it were difficult to enforce while others took time to put into place. The time taken to enforce all the legislation meant the Children's Charter only helped improve conditions for some children during the period from 1906 to 1914.

The Old

Seebohm Rowntree was only one of many social reformers who argued that something should be done to help the poor who were doomed to become even poorer when they became too old to work. Charles Booth had earlier recommended old-age pensions and as Lloyd George, Chancellor of the Exchequer said:

> "
> *It is rather a shame... to allow those who have toiled all their days to end in penury and possibly starvation. It is rather hard that an old workman should have to find his way to the gates of the tomb... through the brambles and thorns of poverty. The provision for the aged and deserving poor – it was time it was done.*

Lloyd George believed the best way of helping was to guarantee an income to people who were too old to work, and this was done in 1908 with the Old Age Pensions Act. People over 70 were given between 1 shilling (5 pence) and 5 shillings (25 pence) a week depending on any income they might have. Once a person over 70 had income above 12 shillings (60 pence) a week, their entitlement to a pension stopped. Married couples were given 7 shillings and 6 pence (37 pence). The Liberals hailed old age pensions as a great success.

A description of an old lady collecting her pension at the post office and saying, 'Thank goodness for that Lord George' (she naively thought only someone as great as a Lord could be so generous), taken from Lark Rise to Candleford, is often used to support the claim that old-age pensions were a huge benefit to the poor. Lloyd George himself described the reform as part of a Liberal campaign:

> to wage warfare against poverty and squalidness. I cannot help hoping and believing that before this generation has passed away, we shall have advanced a great step towards that good time, when poverty... will be as remote to the people of this country as the wolves which once infested its forests.

But just how realistic were these claims of success? Rowntree's own study had identified the bare minimum income to stop a person from falling below his primary poverty line was 7 shillings (35 pence) a week and a married couple required 11 shillings and 8 pence (58 pence). Clearly the old-age pension came nowhere near meeting the basic needs of the elderly poor.

Labour politicians argued that the level of benefits were too low, and that few of the genuinely poor would live till their 70th birthday. Life expectancy in the worst industrial slums was in the mid-40s, and working people suffered the ageing effects of harsh working and living conditions. By their early 50s most were too old to continue hard physical work.

Many had hoped the pension would be paid to all the elderly but when the details were announced there were complaints that many of the old were excluded from claiming pension because they failed to meet several qualification rules. These rules were that no person who had claimed poor relief in the previous year or had been in prison in the previous two years could claim a pension. Nor could people who had failed to work regularly.

It can easily be argued that the amounts of money given as a pension were not enough to prevent poverty, but by 1914 there were 970,000 claimants. The Old Age Pensions Act may not have solved the problem of poverty for the elderly but it did make life slightly better.

Source 4.11

In this photo Lloyd George is being welcomed by old people, presumably grateful for the new old age pension.

Helping the sick

In 1911 there was no free National Health Service. The poor could not usually afford medical help especially as they lost wages during absence from work. Illness was recognised as a major cause of poverty.

To ease the problem of poverty through illness or unemployment, the Chancellor of the Exchequer, David Lloyd George, introduced the National Insurance Act which created a system of insurance against illness and unemployment. In 1908 Lloyd George had visited Germany and had seen for himself the German insurance system, established twenty years earlier. He returned convinced of the need to assist workers who had fallen on hard times through no fault of their own. He argued that since Germany, Britain's rival in the years leading to the First World War, could provide a national insurance scheme for its workers, why could Britain not do likewise and put itself on 'a level with Germany, and... not emulate (copy) them only in armaments.'

The 1911 National Insurance Act was in two parts. The first part created a scheme of unemployment insurance and a Labour Exchange scheme. The second part was the health insurance scheme. The money paid was provided by contributions from the person insured, the government and the employer.

The National Insurance Scheme of 1911 applied to workers aged between 16 and 60 earning less than £160 a year – about 15 million people. The scheme was called a contributory system since each worker paid 4 pence a week towards the help they received. The employer paid 3 pence a week and the government paid 2 pence a week. That meant each insured worker got 9 pence in benefits from an outlay of 4 pence. Lloyd George himself popularised the scheme with the slogan, 'ninepence for fourpence'.

An insured worker got ten shillings a week (50 pence) when off sick but the benefits only lasted for 26 weeks. A sickness benefit of 10 shillings (50 pence) per week was paid for 13 weeks. Women received less – only 35 pence. After 13 weeks the benefit was reduced to only 5 shillings (25 pence) a week for a further 13 weeks. Other help for insured workers was a 30 shillings (£1.50) maternity grant and free medical treatment including medicines.

Source 4.12

The National Insurance Act provided real help for workers facing difficulties through ill health or unemployment.

Those workers who contributed were also guaranteed 7 shillings a week for fifteen weeks in any one year when they were unemployed. The benefits were paid at the recently opened Labour Exchanges, which also provided unemployed workers with information on any vacancies which existed in the area.

How helpful was the National Insurance Act?

Illness and absence from work was the major cause of poverty, therefore any money coming in as 'sick pay insurance benefit' would help a family during hard times. But the new law was limited in its help.

Firstly, only the insured worker got free medical treatment from a doctor. Other family members did not benefit from the scheme, no matter how sick they were. Nor did the scheme apply to the self-employed or the slightly better paid, or to treatment by dentists or opticians. The fact that this scheme did not cover hospital treatment, except admission to the sanatorium intended to benefit tuberculosis sufferers, increased the risk of poverty.

The limited time in which benefits were paid was a difficulty and the government did attempt to improve the scheme by abolishing the reduced benefits for the second 13-week period in favour of the full benefit for a period of 26 weeks. This was an improvement but many workers were sick for longer than this.

Finally, the fact that this scheme was self-contributory reduced its success. The weekly contributions of 4 pennies (about 2 pence) was in effect a wage cut which might simply have made poverty worse in many families.

Helping the unemployed

William Beveridge, an advisor to Lloyd George, argued forcibly that 'The problem of unemployment lies at the root of most other social problems.'

The National Insurance Act Part 2 tried to ease the problem of temporary unemployment but unlike Part 1 of the act, which dealt with health insurance for all workers, Part 2 only covered unemployment for some workers in some industries, specifically building and construction, shipbuilding, mechanical engineering, iron-founding, construction of vehicles and sawmilling. These industries were thought to be most liable to varying employment levels at different times of the year.

In effect unemployment insurance only covered 2.25 million workers and, like Part 1 of the act, required contributions from workers, employers and the government. In 1912 Beveridge described how the system operated:

> *Every worker in those trades had to have an unemployment booklet. Each week the employer had to attach an insurance stamp which cost 5 pence. Half of that amount ($2\frac{1}{2}$ pence) was deducted from the worker's wages. The government also contributed $2\frac{1}{2}$ pence per worker. The benefit was 7 shillings a week up to a maximum of fifteen weeks. The worker claimed and received benefit at an unemployment exchange. He proved his unemployment and his capacity to work by signing an unemployment register there in working hours daily.*

Was the scheme helpful?

The help provided by this scheme was useful to the worker, as it meant they were not immediately poor if they became unemployed. With 15 weeks to look for work there was a good chance the worker would not face a long time without income. The new Labour Exchanges also made finding new work much easier.

On the other hand, while in work insured workers had an enforced pay cut as their contributions bit into weekly wages, and they were only insured for 15 weeks, which meant after this period they would have no financial support even if hit by long-term unemployment. Workers who were already poor when this scheme was introduced were not helped by it. There was no difference between a married or single worker. Rather, a worker was maintained in poverty, suffered a poverty level benefit if unemployed, then after 15 weeks faced no help at all. And for most workers, no unemployment insurance scheme existed.

The system rested on the assumption that unemployment levels would never rise above 5% of the workforce. This meant that contributions from those in work would easily cover the benefit paid out to those unemployed. That is what Beveridge meant by describing the system as self-financing. But could the system survive if unemployment rose above 10%, as happened after the First World War?

Working conditions

It can be argued that the Liberal government's reforms were a direct result of a determination among certain Liberal ministers such as Lloyd George and Winston Churchill to prevent the working classes from supporting the new Labour Party. This is particularly true of the reforms to improve working conditions, but again there were serious limitations in what was achieved.

In 1906 the Liberals extended an earlier Workman's Compensation Act to cover a further six million workers who could now claim compensation for injuries and diseases which were the result of working conditions.

However in many trades and industries the government failed to establish minimum wage levels or a limit to working hours, thereby doing little to ease poverty for many workers.

On the other hand there were exceptions for specific trades. In 1908, miners secured an eight-hour working day, the first time the length of the working day was fixed for adult men. In 1909, the Trade Boards Act tried to protect workers in the sweated trades like tailoring and lace making, by setting up trade boards to fix minimum wages. Two years later, in 1911, a Shops Act limited working hours and guaranteed a half-day closing for shop assistants.

The introduction of Labour Exchanges in 1909 has been welcomed by historians as a genuine attempt to help workers find jobs and minimise the time out of work for many workers. Labour Exchanges, similar to today's job centres, opened all over the country. There, unemployed people could register and employers with vacancies could enquire about suitable workers. However, other historians argue that the introduction of Labour Exchanges was ineffective as work was still very hard to find and wages were low. Labour Exchanges might help a worker to find a different low-paid job but in the longer term it is argued they did little to pull workers over the poverty line.

How effective were the Liberal reforms?

The Liberal reforms eased the problem of poverty for the young, sick, unemployed and old. They also attempted to improve the treatment of workers with the introduction of working hours and minimum wages in some industries. It can also be argued that the reforms were as successful as they could have been under the circumstances and given the scale of the poverty problem facing the government when it came to power. It is also the case that the Liberals were distracted by the increasing threat from Germany and the expense of preparing for war, especially the naval race. Finally, the Liberals also had to deal with a mainly Conservative House of Lords which regularly opposed Liberal proposals.

On the other hand the reforms had serious limitations. At a time when inflation was reducing the purchasing power of worker's wages and job insecurity was rising, many workers were unimpressed by the Liberal reforms. The fact that aspects of poverty such as housing were not dealt with by Liberal legislation added to the idea that Liberal reforms 'missed their target' and were not entirely successful in dealing with poverty and need.

Perhaps the best overall comment on the Liberal reforms is that they were very successful at dealing with the situation when considering the huge task they undertook, not just in terms of the poverty of the nation but the need to change attitudes about the government's role in society.

It is certainly true that the Liberal reforms marked a change away from laissez faire to a more interventionist approach, which meant the government took on some responsibility for the welfare of everyone in the nation. But it would be wrong to say the Liberals created a welfare state.

The Liberal reforms marked a transition point, a half-way house, between old laissez-faire attitudes and what was later called the welfare state. Between the years of 1906 and 1914 Liberal governments laid the foundations of a welfare state and Winston Churchill neatly summed up the nature of the Liberal reforms: 'If we see a drowning man we do not drag him to the shore. Instead, we provide help to allow him to swim ashore.' In other words, the Liberals provided some help for the 'deserving poor' in order that they could help themselves.

Why was there such a row over the reforms?

In this section you should be aware how the row that erupted over the Liberal reforms links into other topics such as the growth of democracy and the issue of the power of the House of Lords.

In a democracy, parliament should reflect the wishes of the people. But parliament is made up of the House of Commons and the House of Lords. The members of the House of Lords were not elected, but making the Liberal reforms into law was dependent on the House of Lords approval.

The question of who would pay for the Liberal reforms came to a head in 1909. The government announced its plans to raise taxes to pay for the reforms in its budget, which was called the People's Budget.

Source 4.13

The Liberal reforms were paid for mainly by raising income tax. In this cartoon the word 'milking' is used as another word for robbing or taking more than is deserved. The income tax payer is complaining that the Liberals are taking too much in tax.

CRESCENDO;
OR, THE TUNE THE OLD COW'S LIKELY TO DIE OF.
The Cow. "STOP! STOP! THIS ISN'T MILKING; IT'S MURDER!"

The government proposed to raise taxation on motor tax and alcohol and create a super tax on the very wealthy, who did not like the proposal but since the Liberals were the government there seemed little that could be done. However the House of Lords had the power to veto any suggestion for a new law made by the House of Commons and this is what they did to the budget. If the budget did not become law the Liberals could not raise taxes and so could not pay for the social reforms.

This conflict is essential to the growth of democracy in Britain. Since the elected government of Britain had decided to pass a new law (the budget is a type of law called a Money Bill) what right did the non-elected House of Lords have to stop it? After a long argument and two more elections the Parliament Act of 1911 resolved the situation. The authority of the Lords was restricted since it was the unelected, unaccountable part of parliament.

The Parliament Act of 1911 reduced the power of the House of Lords. It had no say over budgets and could no longer veto bills passed by the House of Commons. They could only be delayed by the Lords for two years.

Activity ▐▐▐➡

You are a researcher working for the Liberal Party just after their election victory in 1906. You have been asked to prepare a report recommending whether or not the party should consider a programme of social reforms.

In your report you should:

- recommend whether or not a programme of social reforms should go ahead.
- provide arguments to support your conclusions.
- identify and comment on any arguments which may be presented by those who oppose your recommendation.
- use extensive background knowledge.

You may be requested to present your report in written form or as a spoken presentation lasting between two and four minutes.

Exam essays 📑

Other essay types in this section could be:

1 'Concern about national security was the real reason for the Liberal reforms.' How far do you agree with this view?

2 To what extent did the Liberal reforms deal effectively with the problem of poverty?

The National Government and the problems of unemployment

Introduction

In Britain the decades of the 1920s and 1930s are associated with economic depression and high levels of unemployment. In particular, the 1930s are often thought of as years of ceaseless gloom and depression. Is that impression fair and accurate? And even if true, could such a situation be true of Britain as a whole?

The focus of this chapter is on how the coalition National Governments of the 1930s tried to cope with the problems of economic depression and mass unemployment.

The main question is how successful the National Governments were in dealing with the economic and social problems facing Britain in the 1930s.

Why was there mass unemployment between the wars?

The roots of the problem go back at least to the end of the Great War. In 1919 Britain was poorer and weaker than it had been in 1914.

The war had also damaged Britain's trading position. During four years of war, trading contacts around the world had been disrupted or lost. Denied British goods, countries around the world had found new suppliers or started producing their own products. By 1920 foreign competition was growing and damaging Britain's trade. Britain's policy of Free Trade allowed foreign goods to enter the country easily, but Britain's competitors often blocked British goods getting into their country. Altogether, British exports during the 1920s were about 80% of their pre-war levels and there was little chance of Britain being able to rebuild its former levels of overseas investment.

The decline in British exports hit the old traditional industries such as coalmining, shipbuilding and steel. Britain had become too dependent on these old traditional industries, which were known collectively as 'staple industries' and were located mainly in the North of England, South Wales and Central Scotland. Put simply, with the decline in Britain's share of world trade, less ships were needed for trading, which meant less iron and steel was needed, which in turn cut demand for coal. The result was that the traditional industrial areas of Britain spent the rest of the 1920s in recession, and unemployment in those 'depressed areas' became a large problem. Throughout the 1920s unemployment stayed around one million.

Source 5.1

In 1900 it looked as if industrial jobs would go on unchanged for ever.

Britain's export difficulties were also made worse by the decision to return to the Gold Standard in April 1925. This was a system of interconnecting major world currencies all linked to the value of gold. To exaggerate, if £1 bought one gramme of gold and it cost 4 US dollars to buy one gramme of gold then the exchange rate was fixed between the USA and Britain at £1 being worth 4 US dollars. The Gold Standard was a problem because it locked Britain into an exchange rate which made British exports very expensive. The result was that other countries bought what they needed from new suppliers rather than Britain. To offset the effects of the high exchange rate, the export industries tried to cut costs by lowering workers' wages.

The 1920s did see the development of new industries such as the motor industry and the electrical industry. Unfortunately British products in these areas were not usually sufficiently advanced to compete in world markets against foreign competitors possessing more up-to-date technology, so British products largely served the domestic market. These new industries would become important in the 1930s but in the decade of the 20s they were not enough to solve Britain's unemployment problems. Additionally, the new industries were mainly located in the south of England, while the declining industries were in the north, Scotland and South Wales. The result was that people who lost their jobs were in the wrong part of the country and had the wrong skills to gain new jobs in the new industries.

People who became unemployed often remained out of work for months and years. Workers who have been unemployed for a long time are much less likely to find a job as they begin to lose skills. By the end of the 1920s, people who had been unemployed for more than a year had only a 1% chance of finding a new job. Unemployment had become a serious and continuing problem.

By the end of the 1920s the British economy already faced serious problems. And then the World Depression of 1929–1933 took place!

Crash

In 1929 a new and inexperienced Labour Government took over the running of the country. Almost immediately it was faced with huge economic problems stemming from the economic crash in America in 1929. As economic depression spread from America around the world, British exports fell in value by 50% between 1929 and 1931. Economic problems which had been serious in the 1920s became disastrous after 1929. Unemployment in Britain, which was already over 1 million, shot up to 2.5 million by December 1930. The government seemed unable to reduce it and, lacking in experience, it fell back on traditional ideas about running the economy. These ideas were called 'orthodox' ideas. The core of economic orthodoxy was that governments should always try to balance the books. In other words income must balance spending. So if the nation's income was falling, then the only thing to do, so they believed, was to cut spending.

Cutting spending – the May Report

High unemployment was the most serious problem facing the government. It was never lower than 10% of the labour force between 1920 and 1939, and reached 22% in 1932 – over three million workers. This compares with an unemployment rate before the First World War of about 4%. The system of unemployment insurance started by the Liberals in 1911 was never designed to cope with mass unemployment. As the unemployment figures rose it meant that money paid out of the 'national kitty' through benefits was rising – but rising unemployment also meant that fewer people were paying into the 'kitty'.

Payment of unemployment benefit was placing a severe strain on the government's finances. In 1931 a committee was appointed under Sir George May to investigate national spending and to suggest ways of saving money. The May Report was published in July 1931 and recommended cutting the wages of public sector workers such as members of the armed forces, civil servants and police. Teachers were hit by the largest cut of all, 20%. But the most serious recommendation was that unemployment benefit should also be cut by the same large amount.

MacDonald and the fall of the government, August 1931

Prime Minister Ramsay MacDonald and his Chancellor of the Exchequer Philip Snowden accepted the May Report's recommendations, although unemployment benefit was only cut by 10%. But even this was too much for many Labour politicians. They asked why a party of the working-class, based on socialist principles, should impose benefit cuts which would cause serious poverty just to keep a capitalist system alive. On a personal level, were not the cuts being aimed at the very people who had voted Labour in 1929?

After a fierce argument in the cabinet, 10 out of its 21 members refused to accept any cuts in unemployment benefit. This split caused MacDonald to hand in the government's resignation. The date was August 1931.

When the Labour government fell in August 1931 there was a desire for a strong government to deal with the economic, social and financial problems arising from the Great Depression. As The Times reported:

Source 5.2

By the end of the 1920s unemployment was a serious problem affecting all of Scotland's industries.

> *The Prime Minister yesterday handed in the resignation of the Government to the King who entrusted Mr MacDonald with the task of forming a National Government for the sole purpose of meeting the present financial emergency.*
>
> *The Times, 25 August 1931.*

The Labour Party, still divided over the issue of spending cuts, was shocked. While The Times report was a factual record of events, an account by Philip Snowden, Chancellor of the Exchequer, revealed the anger, surprise and emotion involved in the creation of the new coalition National Government.

> *Mr MacDonald agreed to the formation of a National Government, with himself as Prime Minister, without a word of previous consultation with any of his Labour colleagues… This was naturally taken as an indication that he had finally separated himself from the Party and did not want its support.*

The new National Government took power in August 1931. Although MacDonald remained prime minister, the Conservatives had control of the new government because they had a majority of MPs. MacDonald was kept

The National Government and the problems of unemployment

on as a symbol of continuity and unity. It was also thought that he might attract working-class support for the new government, although given the feeling that MacDonald had betrayed his party such support was unlikely.

The National Government was formed to combat the Great Depression and between 1931 and 1935 economic issues were the government's top priority.

The National Government in action

Spending cuts

The National Government immediately cut spending in line with the suggestions of the May Report. They believed that financial stability and 'balanced books' would restore the confidence of foreign investors in Britain. Income tax was raised, the wages of public employees such as civil servants, the police and teachers were cut by 10% and so too was unemployment benefit, also by 10%. A short-lived mutiny by sailors at Invergordon, angered by the cuts, temporarily scared the government but the problem faded when the sailors were assured there would be no more cuts in their wages.

Devaluation

Although the National Government struggled to maintain 'economic orthodoxy' the old symbol of Britain's financial strength – the Gold Standard – was a victim of the financial crisis. The Gold Standard was abandoned in 1931 with the result that the value of the pound in relation to other currencies was reduced. This is called devaluing the pound.

Apart from losing pride, the real effect was to make exports cheaper since it cost other countries less to buy British products. However, in the depths of worldwide economic depression and a trade slump, British exports increased only slightly.

Protection and tariffs

Government thinking now turned towards protecting British trade from foreign competition. Britain's trading policy had been based on free trade, which meant that imports could enter Britain without restrictions and could compete freely with British-made products. However, with rising unemployment, the government believed that by putting duties (like a tax or tariff) on imported goods, demand for British-made products would increase, since the duty would increase the price of foreign goods. The policy was called protection, since by adding a tax or duty to the import price British goods would be protected from foreign competition.

Of course there was a risk – what if foreign competitors then imposed restrictions on British exports to their countries? Before this policy was adopted, Prime Minister MacDonald called for a General Election. His appeal was for 'a doctor's mandate' to do whatever was necessary for recovery, including the ending of free trade and the introduction of tariffs.

Stanley Baldwin, in the Conservative/National Government manifesto of 1931 recognised what had been achieved but prepared the way for an end to free trade:

> It is barely two months since my decision to join the National Government. The Budget has been balanced. But we are not yet earning enough to pay for what we have to buy from overseas.
>
> This can be accomplished only be reducing imports, by increasing exports, or by a combination of both. I shall continue to press upon the electors that in my view the tariff is the quickest and most effective weapon not only to reduce excessive imports but to enable us to induce other countries to lower their tariff walls.
>
> — *Stanley Baldwin, 1931.*

By the end of 1931 temporary restrictions were put on some imports and the following year at the Imperial Conference in Ottawa, Canada, Britain and its empire made agreements about their mutual trade arrangements. However, the agreements reached did not work to Britain's advantage as much as the government had hoped. In effect a system of preference was given which meant that British goods would be cheaper to buy within the empire than those from non-empire countries.

Officially, free trade was abandoned by the Import Duties Act of 1932 which placed a 10% duty on most imports, except those from the countries in the British Empire. The result of the Ottawa Conference was that during the rest of the 1930s Britain's trade was directed much more towards the empire but the overall level of trade was not boosted. This policy, of which so much had been expected, turned out to be of only limited importance.

Cheap money

One policy of the National Government which is credited with encouraging economic recovery from the depression was 'cheap money'. Quite simply cheap money meant keeping interest rates low so it was relatively cheap to borrow money. Whether you were an ordinary house buyer trying to get a mortgage or a large business wanting to borrow money to expand, loans were fairly easy to get and low interest rates meant they were easy to repay.

After the National Government took over, interest rates were kept at 2%. This low rate did help recovery and led to a house-building boom as many people realised for the first time that they could afford to buy their own

homes. Between 1932 and 1934 house building increased greatly and that in turn boosted demand for supplies such as bricks, concrete, timber and electrical goods and tradesmen to build and equip the houses. If the extra jobs in these industries are included, house building accounted for one-third of all economic growth during 1932–35.

However, low interest rates did not encourage recovery everywhere. Borrowers had to be in secure long term work and confident about their future prospects. Businesses had to be sure they could sell what they produced. As a result, the policy of cheap money did little to help the depressed areas. In those places the scarcity of long-term secure employment and the difficulty of selling what was produced even before expanding a business discouraged borrowing even at 'cheap' interest rates.

Source 5.3

The goverment's policy of low interst rates led to a housing boom but did little to help the long-term problems in depressed areas.

Unemployment – the overview

There were really two unemployment problems in the 1930s – a short-term and a long-term problem. Short-term unemployment was not new to Britain. It was often called cyclical unemployment because after a time of economic slump the economy would automatically pick up. These trade cycles of good times followed by bad then followed by good had happened for decades. But what was not realised in the 1920s was that British industry was facing problems which would not simply go away after a short time. Instead, Britain was facing long-term structural unemployment in the old traditional industries, caused mainly by weaknesses or problems in the structure of the industry, such as a failure to modernise or an increase in more efficient foreign competition.

What industries suffered most?

Throughout the 1920s there was a steady growth of structural unemployment, even before the impact of the World Economic Crisis after 1929, which added cyclical unemployment to the structural problems already faced by shipbuilding, iron and steel making, coal mining and textiles. These industries had been powerful creators of wealth in the 19th century and were known as Britain's traditional industries. By the end of the 1920s, over half the total of Britain's unemployed had worked in those industries.

In 1931 the Report of the Royal Commission on Unemployment Insurance described the problem.

> *The causes of the depression in the industries of exceptional unemployment are easy to understand. There is first, the class of industry which is still suffering from a wartime expansion in excess of normal peace-time requirements ... In this class fall iron and steel, shipbuilding, and to some extent coal mining. Second, the class of industry that before the war was dependent to a great extent on exports, this accounts for the exceptional unemployment in the textile and coal mining industries.*
>
> Report of the Royal Commission on Unemployment Insurance, 1931.

Where was unemployment most serious?

Although unemployment was the major economic and social problem of the interwar years it was not a problem suffered equally across the country. Scotland, Northern Ireland, North-East England and South Wales were areas reliant on the old traditional industries and in Scotland the unemployment rate stood at over 20%. In Wales it was around 30%.

Source 5.4

Unemployment remained a serious problem for the government. This election poster suggests things were getting better by 1935, and they were.

On the other hand, the south of England and the Midlands benefited from the rapid growth of newer industries such as motorcars, aircraft and chemicals along with large-scale house building. Between 1929 and 1936 their unemployment rate was around 8%.

The effects of long-term unemployment

By the early 1930s unemployment rose to over 3 million workers. In the areas of old traditional industries people were out of work for months and years. Areas of high unemployment became bleak areas as shops and other businesses where workers had spent their wages were forced to close down. Families fell into debt and many were evicted for non-payment of rent. Diet suffered and health deteriorated. There was an increase in diseases and prolonged unemployment sometimes led to depression and mental disorders. In Jarrow, North-East England, the local MP Ellen Wilkinson described the problem.

> "
> *No one had a job except a few railwaymen, officials, the workers in the co-operative stores, and a few workmen who went out of the town... the plain fact [is] that if people have to live and bear and bring up their children in bad houses on too little food, their resistance to disease is lowered and they die before they should.*
>
> Ellen Wilkinson, The Town that was Murdered, 1939.

What could be done to reduce unemployment?

The government was faced by a huge problem. In 1910 government expenditure on unemployment had been nil. By 1925 spending had risen to £16.9 million. By 1930 that sum had increased to £50 million. As income from the contributions of insured workers fell, and payments to those same workers who were now unemployed increased, the government was faced with difficult choices. What would happen when an insured worker's entitlement to payments ended? And what about the thousands of long term uninsured workers?

What did the government do?

The Special Areas Act of 1934 appointed unpaid commissioners to encourage economic development in depressed areas. For example, new firms were encouraged to set up in depressed areas and trading estates, such as at North Hillington and Larkhall, near Glasgow, were built.

However, there were strict rules about what areas qualified to be called 'special'. The unemployment rate had to be above 25% of the insured population, and over 40% of the insured workers had to work in the same industry. Clydebank was a special area but Glasgow, with a 'low' unemployment rate of nearly 37% spread over several industries, did not qualify.

One well-publicised success which did help Clydebank was the launching of the passenger ship, the Queen Mary.

The Queen Mary

Shipbuilding on the river Clyde faced serious problems as the depression became worse. In 1930 John Brown's shipyard on the Clyde had announced a new passenger ship was to be built but by 1932 the economic depression had hit the shipbuilding industry, building stopped and the Clydebank workforce was laid off indefinitely.

Eventually, in December 1933, a government loan of £9.5 million was agreed and in April 1934 work resumed on the ship. The work was completed in March 1936 and the completion of the Queen Mary remains one of the most famous examples of government help to a traditional industry in a depressed area. Shipbuilding on the Clyde was certainly helped by government intervention but the story of the Queen Mary also demonstrated just how dependent the depressed areas of the country were on a handful of older industries facing serious difficulties.

The Special Areas Act had very limited success. Even the government recognised their actions were not wholly successful when their manifesto of 1935 declared, 'No branch of the Government's activities has been more constantly misrepresented that their work in the Special Areas. From the first they have recognised that in these areas – the unfortunate victims of a contraction in the limited number of great industries on which they were formerly chiefly dependent – the problems of unemployment present features of exceptional difficulty.'

The two commissioners appointed in 1934 resigned in 1936, arguing that government funding was not enough and employers could not be forced to move into the depressed areas. Between 1934 and 1938, the commissioners spent £9m and created around 50,000 jobs. About 44,000 workers were encouraged to move to other towns and 30,000 men were found places on retraining courses. However, unemployment in the 'special areas' totalled 362,000 in 1935, a huge problem to solve with limited resources.

Source 5.5

The building of the Queen Mary in 1934 at Clydebank provided thousands of jobs in an area severely hit by the economic depression.

What was done for the unemployed?

The system of unemployment insurance had changed slightly since the Liberal reforms of 1911 but it was still dependent on money coming in from insured workers building up a fund of money which would pay for those out of work. It was never designed to cope with massive unemployment.

Unemployment benefit lasted for 26 weeks and when this time was up, people were given transitional payments. George Orwell in *The Road to Wigan Pier* described the arrangements for unemployment benefit.

> *When a man is first unemployed, until his insurance stamps are exhausted, he draws 'full benefit', which was less than £1 although money was added for dependants under 14. A family of three gets just under 30 shillings(£1.50) each week.*
>
> *When a man's stamps are exhausted, before being turned over to the Public Assistance Committee, he receives twenty-six weeks' 'transitional benefit' from the Unemployment Assistance Board.*
>
> George Orwell, The Road to Wigan Pier.

The Unemployment Assistance Board was created in 1934 and was responsible for the long-term unemployed. The UAB paid out benefits after an unemployed man ran out of the normal period of insurance benefit. The relief given, however, was linked to the hated household Means Test, introduced in 1931.

The Means Test took into account the total family income and any savings put aside for a rainy day when assessing the amount of relief to be received. To many unemployed workers, it seemed their dignity was being stripped from them and those who had struggled to save were being punished by getting less help. In some cases unemployed men were dependent on their daughters or

Source 5.6

George Orwell's *Road to Wigan Pier* captures the feelings of people living through the depression years.

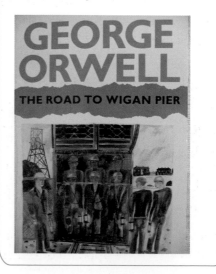

wives, a situation that did not fit in with the social customs of the time. In Walter Greenwood's *Love on the Dole*, family hopes and plans were destroyed by the Means Test when, 'Harry Hardcastle was informed that his dole was to stop because his father's dole and his sister Sally's meagre earnings were considered sufficient to keep him. His vision of getting married and setting up home was shattered at a blow.'

Unemployed workers also had to prove they were actively seeking work, otherwise their benefit would be cut. Ewan McCall described the soul-destroying experience of men standing in line in places where jobs were available, knowing full well there was no realistic chance of getting employment but needing the proof that they were 'actively seeking work'.

> *The queue of applicants for this job must have numbered close on a hundred. In the short time that I stood there, another thirty or forty lined up behind me. We stood there and shuffled slowly up the steps and through the entrance to the offices where two young men wielding rubber-stamps put the firm's mark on our chits, proof that we'd actually followed the Labour Exchange's instructions in applying for the job.*
>
> Ewan McColl, *A Political Journey*.

To be fair, the government was in an impossible position. The contributory system of unemployment insurance started by the Liberals had collapsed in the face of long-term unemployment. The cost of paying benefit to the unemployed was huge and a way had to be found to cut that amount. In defence of the Means Test, the government recognised the problem in its 1935 manifesto.

> *As regards the Means Test, the Government believe that no responsible person would seriously suggest that Unemployment Assistance, which is not insurance benefit, ought to be paid without regard to the resources properly available to the applicant. The question is not whether there should be a Means Test, but what that test should be.*

The Jarrow March

In 1936, mass unemployment and extreme poverty in the north-east of England drove 200 men to march in protest from Jarrow to London. They wanted parliament, and the people in the south, to understand that they were ordinary people facing long-term unemployment which affected 70% of the work force and their families. The marchers carried with them a petition signed by 11,000 Jarrow residents.

The marchers were carefully chosen. Men were medically examined, and 200 fit men were appointed to march, starting at 8.45 each morning and

The National Government and the problems of unemployment

walking for 25 days. A bus carried cooking equipment, and arrangements were made for overnight stops, either in accommodation provided by sympathetic supporters or in the open air.

One helper along the route described how, on one occasion, he saw a marcher take the ham from inside his sandwich, and place it in an envelope. When asked what he was doing he replied, 'I'm sending it home … my family haven't had meat in the house for six weeks.'

Was the march a success?

Despite considerable public sympathy the march made little real impact. Perhaps they were too polite. They caused no disruption and relied on their petition and the persuasive powers of their charismatic MP, Ellen Wilkinson, who presented their petition on 4th November. In response to a request to meet, Prime Minister Stanley Baldwin sent a message that he was too busy to meet any of the marchers.

Bad times or boom times?

To assess 'The Hungry Thirties' as a time of depression and failed government policies is to ignore the fact that for most Britons it was not a time of gloom and depression. From 1932 onwards, southern Britain entered a time of prosperity and growth. After 1931 unemployment fell and although unemployment remained high, for those workers who remained in work during the 1930s there was a big improvement in living standards. In the 1930s prices of goods fell, with the result that wages bought more. Economists call that a rise in real wages – what wages could really buy. As the recovery continued after 1935, the majority of the population began to enjoy a higher standard of living than ever before.

In 1899 Seebohm Rowntree had carried out his famous investigation into poverty in York. In 1936 he returned. He found that the lives of the population had improved greatly. The reasons, he suggested, included the rise in real wages, the fall in the size of families and the large increase in government intervention, covering issues such as health and unemployment insurance. Even for the poor, life was better than 30 years before.

Almost 3 million houses were built in the 1930s. Expansion of housing gave a boost to many industries providing furnishings and electrical

Source 5.7

The Jarrow crusade was the most famous of many hunger marches trying to bring attention to the desperate problems of unemployment.

equipment, such as electric cookers and refrigerators. The numbers of cars doubled in the 1930s and the number of radios sold trebled. Holidays with pay became a reality for most families in the 1930s and more fresh fruit, vegetables and dairy produce was eaten, helping to improve the health of the nation.

For those in continuous work the 1930s were far from hungry and depressed. It was a different story in the depressed areas. Recovery was a long way off. There was no big housing boom and consumer goods, if they existed on shop shelves, remained unsold. Exports failed to regain previous levels and unemployment still remained a problem. The structural problems in Britain's old traditional industries remained unsolved. In Jarrow, a new ship-breaking yard and engineering works were established in 1938 and the Consett Iron Company started a steelworks in 1939.

From 1936 onwards the rearmament programme helped in the creation of extra jobs and the government recognised the beneficial effects of rearmament on depressed areas in its 1935 election manifesto.

Source 5.8

In the 1930s, southern areas of Britain enjoyed increasing prosperity. Away from the depressed areas some people in work could buy a new motor car. The new car industry also provided jobs. But £150 was about 25 times the weekly wage – the equivalent of £10,000 today.

> It may be observed that the new orders required for defence purposes will undoubtedly bring a considerable volume of work and employment into some parts of the country which hitherto have been most hard hit by the heavy depression, and most backward in feeling the general improvement which has been manifest (obvious) elsewhere.

Conclusion

The traditional view of the National Government is that it neither helped nor hampered the economy. Recovery was probably due more to favourable circumstances than to the efforts of the National Government.

The crisis that fell on Britain in the early 1930s fell on the shoulders of politicians who Churchill described as 'decided only to be undecided' and who consciously opted for a strategy of 'safety first' and put their emphasis on the avoidance of economic collapse.

On the other hand, more recent opinions on the National Government's response to the socio-economic problems of the period lean towards the view that very little could have been done to prevent the structural problems experienced by the traditional industries and the subsequent problems associated with massive unemployment.

Policies of protection, cheap money, and the Special Areas policy all assisted recovery, but together they do not explain why Britain pulled out of the slump. New industries carried the flag of recovery as did returning confidence, helped no doubt by the policy of cheap money. But as in the USA, real recovery only arrived as a result of external factors pushing Britain towards war. In 1939, the year war broke out again, there were still 1.5 million people unemployed.

Activity ▐▐▐▶

Work in pairs or a group of three.

- Design **three** word searches, each one no larger than 10 squares by 10 squares.
- One of your puzzles must only contain words or phrases linked to the main themes or issues in this chapter.
- Your second puzzle must only contain words or phrases linked to the actions of the National Government.
- Your third puzzle must only contain names of significant people in this chapter.
- The words/phrases can go in any direction and phrases can be split.
- Each word/phrase must have a definition or clue to help someone find the words/phrases.
- When you have completed your puzzle exchange it with another group or person and use the clues to the puzzle you received to find the answers.

Exam essays 🗐

Other essay types in this section could be:

1 Why did the National Government face such serious economic and social problems in the early 1930s?

2 'Too little and too late'. Do you agree with this assessment of the actions of the National Government in response to the social and economic problems facing Britain after 1931?

6 Labour and the Welfare State 1945–1951

Introduction

Between 1945 and 1951 a series of social reforms were put into operation by the Labour government which established a welfare state in Britain, in which the government took responsibility for the well being of its citizens 'from the cradle to the grave'.

The experience of war between 1939 and 1945 had prepared the public for greater government intervention in their lives and had created a commonly-felt attitude that 'post-war had to be better than pre-war'. A deluge of government information office films shown in cinemas promoted the idea of a new Britain after the war. In the words of one such film, The Dawn Guard, made in 1941, 'there must be no going back to the lines of men looking for work and no back-to-back housing with no toilets neither.'

As the general election of August 1945 approached, Labour issued their manifesto – their vision of what a post-war Britain would look like. It was entitled 'Let us face the future' and has been described as a 'peaceful revolution'. Some historians, however, believe that far from being a creation of the Labour Party and a social revolution it was heavily based on the achievements of previous governments, especially the Liberals of 1906–1914, the National Government of the 1930s and the wartime coalition government between 1940 and 1945. Those who support this point of view describe Labour's achievements as evolutionary, rather than revolutionary.

Source 6.1

In 1945 Labour won the general election. They promised a bright new future.

AND NOW – WIN THE PEACE

What welfare help existed before 1945?

The Labour government, led by Clement Attlee, is often credited with establishing a welfare state 'from cradle to grave' in Britain where all citizens were provided with a 'safety net' of support through which none should fall into poverty. However, in 1939, before war broke out, Britain already had an established network of welfare help aimed at assisting those in need. National Insurance schemes, started in 1911 and adapted later, covered most manual workers. The long-term unemployed could expect some level of help from the Unemployment Assistance Board. Government-funded schools were in every town and village and even antenatal clinics were increasing. Before war broke out millions of children received free milk in school.

On the other hand it would not be fair to suggest a welfare state for all existed before 1939.

Government-funded benefits were not available for all and the level of support varied from place to place across Britain. State help was only intended for the poorest sections of the community and means tests existed to prove the level of need. Those people above the basic level of need were still expected to pay their doctor's bills, save for their old age and pay the cost of their children's education. Mary McNeil, a 21 year old when war broke out, remembers how it was a common wedding present to have all teeth extracted by a dentist whether they were decayed or not. She said, 'now I wouldn't have to worry about toothache or paying dentist bills when we didn't have much money as young marrieds.'

A good argument can be made in claiming that the experience of World War Two paved the way for the later social reforms and the establishment of a welfare state. The government organised the rationing of food, clothing and fuel and gave extra milk and meals to expectant mothers and children. Evacuation of poor children from inner city areas to the suburbs alerted the middle classes of Britain to the real poverty that still existed

Source 6.2

Clement Attlee was the new Labour Prime Minister. His dream was to create a better society in Britain.

in the industrial slums. Bombing of cities created vast areas which had to be rebuilt, while free hospital treatment for war wounded, including bomb injuries for civilians, and free immunisation are examples of the moves towards a free health service before 1945. To pay for these services the public got used to very high taxation levels with half of every wage packet vanishing as tax to pay for the increased government spending.

Why was the Beveridge Report important?

In late 1942 a battle was fought in the North African deserts. Its name was El Alamein and it was hugely important. For the first time a British Army had inflicted a severe defeat on Nazi plans and although years of war stretched ahead, British people began to realise the war was winnable and they looked ahead to what a new post-war Britain might be like.

Even official announcements from the government promoted the idea that post-war could, and would, be better than pre-war, such as a Ministry of Health statement which referred to 'increasing thought for the future' and that there could be 'no return to the pre-war position.'

Although several plans for the future were suggested for 'social reconstruction' after the war the most important was the Beveridge Report, published in 1942. The report identified five main causes of hardship and poverty. Beveridge called them 'the Five Giants' blocking the path to progress. These giants were **Want** (poverty), **Disease** (bad health), **Squalor** (bad housing), **Ignorance** (poor education) and **Idleness** (unemployment).

Source 6.3

The Beveridge Report, published in 1942, was hugely popular.
The British people hoped that 'post-war would be better than pre-war'.

SOCIAL SECURITY

Here's to the brave new world!

Labour and the Welfare State 1945–1951

Beveridge said 'this is a time for revolution not for patching' and he proposed a universal welfare plan that should cover the whole population of the country. The benefits to be paid out were a right, not a charity or based on a means test.

The main aim of the report was the abolition of Want. Beveridge proposed a scheme of social insurance that would guarantee help for everyone in the event of sickness, unemployment, or any other difficulty which resulted in loss of income. Beveridge also argued that his social insurance plan could only succeed as part of a comprehensive social policy which included family allowances, a National Health Service, and the prevention of mass unemployment. In other words Beveridge argued that all five giants must be defeated if his report was to be successful.

Source 6.4

Sir William Beveridge identified five giant problems facing Britain. His report formed the basis of Labour's social policy between 1945 and 1951.

Even before Labour won the 1945 election, the coalition government of wartime Britain had accepted the main ideas of Beveridge as a way forward for Britain. They accepted Beveridge's plan for a unified and universal scheme, and committed themselves to the creation of a comprehensive National Health Service free at the point of treatment. The Family Allowances Act of 1945, a coalition measure, introduced a child allowance of five shillings a week (25p) for the second and all subsequent children, regardless of family income. The wartime coalition was also concerned that there should be no return to high levels of unemployment, and a White Paper on employment policy, published in 1944, accepted that future governments should maintain a 'high and stable level of employment'.

Turning to education, Beveridge had little to suggest, despite identifying ignorance as one of the giants. Nevertheless, even before Labour won the election, the 1944 Education Act stated that all children over the age of 11 should receive a separate secondary education free of charge and that the school-leaving age was to be raised as soon as possible to 15.

In conclusion, many social reforms were either in place or proposed long before Labour was swept to power and claimed to establish a welfare state. On the other hand, the Labour Party conference of 1942, which met before the Beveridge Report came out, committed a future Labour government to a comprehensive social security scheme, family allowances and a National Health Service. The debate about the influence of the Labour Party in the welfare state established from 1945 on still continues.

Tackling the 'Giants' – Want

In his report, Beveridge had identified want, or poverty, as the main social problem, or giant, to overcome. To do that, the 1946 National Insurance Act created the structure of the welfare state. It extended the original 1911 National Insurance Act to cover all adults and also put into operation a comprehensive National Health Service, effective from 5th July 1948. The Act created a compulsory contributory scheme for every worker and in return for the weekly contribution from workers, employers and government, an individual was entitled to sickness and unemployment benefit, old age pensions for women at 60 and men at 65, widows' and orphans' pensions, and maternity and death grants. James Griffiths, the Minister of National Insurance, described the national insurance scheme as 'the best and cheapest insurance policy offered to the British people, of any people anywhere.' However, weekly contributions took up about 5% of average earnings and people joining the insurance scheme for the first time were not entitled to full pension benefits for ten years. The pensions themselves were still not enough to live on. Despite the Labour government deciding to raise old age pensions to a new level at once, instead of phasing in the increase over twenty years as Beveridge had recommended, by the time the new rates were introduced in 1948 their value had been reduced by inflation. Pension levels remained below basic subsistence levels.

But what about those people not in work or who had not paid enough contributions to qualify for full benefit? A National Assistance Act helped them. People in need could apply for further assistance from National Assistance Boards. This was a break from the past since although applicants were means tested, the money for the extra assistance was provided by the government from taxation, and was not a matter for local administration. Central government even went further in asserting their influence by requiring local authorities to provide homes and other welfare services for the elderly and handicapped. Together with the National Insurance Act, this measure provided a whole new social security structure and really did provide a safety net through which no person should fall into serious poverty.

A Family Allowance Act was also passed to attack household poverty, although this had been started by the wartime government. A small amount of money was paid to all mothers of two or more children. There was no attempt to 'target' the money by means tests and significantly the money

Labour and the Welfare State 1945–1951

was not paid to the fathers but to the mothers, who it was felt were more likely to spend the money on what the children and the household needed.

Finally, an Industrial Injuries Act of 1946 was a big improvement on previous legislation, under which it had been difficult and expensive for a workman to prove that an injury or disability had been caused by his job. Now compensation was paid by the government, not individual employers, and all workers were covered.

Almost 50 years earlier, Seebohm Rowntree had identified old age, sickness, injury at work and unemployment as the main causes of poverty. Labour had directly attacked these problems and

Family allowances were paid directly to mothers and were a big part in Labour's attack on the giant problem of want.

provided help and assurance to many and in so doing removed the fear of falling into serious long-term poverty.

The National Health Service

Possibly because it still exists and affects the lives of everyone, most people consider the greatest achievement of the post-war Labour government to be the creation of a National Health Service. Beginning on July 5 1948, it was based on three main aims. There would be universal access – meaning that the NHS was for everybody. It would be comprehensive, meeting all demands and treating all medical problems. Finally, it was to be free at the point of use. No patient would be asked to pay for any treatment. In reality, of course, the service was and is paid for by the taxation and National Insurance payments made by every worker.

Before 5 July 1948 most health care had to be paid for. About half the male workforce was entitled to assistance through various insurance schemes, although their wives and families did not qualify. Many families had no such insurance and in times of illness had to rely for support on friends and neighbours or local charities.

The NHS offered free health care at the point of need. It entitled everybody, free of charge, to medical care from GPs, specialists and dentists, to spectacles and false teeth and to maternity and child welfare services.

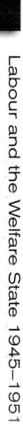

Source 6.6

In 1948 the NHS started. This photo shows Nye Bevan as he launched his masterplan by meeting NHS patients.

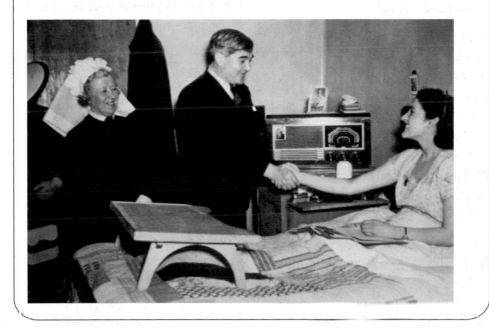

At first there was opposition to the scheme from doctors who resented, as they said, 'being treated like civil servants' and 90% of the members of the British Medical Association threatened to boycott the new scheme. Minister for Health Bevan defused the system with a new method of payments to doctors with the result that when the NHS started on 5 July, 90% of all GPs took part.

The biggest difficulty with the NHS was, and remains, its huge cost. Demand for NHS services surprised everyone. The extent of ill-health among the population had not been realised. It would soon have very serious consequences as the NHS budget rose from the £134m predicted for its establishment in 1948 to £228m in 1949 and £356m in 1950. Remember that at this time Britain was only slowly recovering from the war, with huge demands on government spending. The running expenses of the NHS were reduced slightly but only at the cost of abandoning a key principle of the NHS. In 1951 adults were charged half the cost of false teeth and spectacles. Some Labour politicians, including Bevan himself, resigned in protest at this breaking of the key principle of 'free at point of use'.

In the 1970s historians Sked and Cook in their book *Post-War Britain*, described the NHS as an 'almost revolutionary social innovation since it improved the quality of life of most of the British people; ... it was soon to become the social institution of which the British would feel most proud.'

Labour and the Welfare State 1945–1951

Source 6.7

The Ministry of Health tried to persuade people to adopt a healthier lifestyle under the slogan 'Prevention is better than cure'. They are still doing this.

On the other hand, according to Charles Webster, the official historian of the NHS writing in the late 1980s, 'The NHS failed to improve the general medical service available to the bulk of the population. The middle classes benefited to some extent but the lower classes, especially after the introduction of the prescription charge in 1952, continued to receive an inferior service, but for a higher level of payment through taxes and direct charges.'

Regardless of the debate over the NHS, it remains an important symbol of the brave new world of welfare reforms launched by Labour after 1945.

Education

Beveridge made few direct comments about the giant of ignorance in his report, but he made clear his desire for an education system available to all, especially the poor, which would provide opportunities and develop talent.

Before 1939 education services varied across the country. Although elementary, or primary, education had been established for some time, the quality of secondary education was variable. Many children received no education past primary stage and poorer parents could not afford the fees that some secondary schools charged. Even if a working-class child was given a scholarship to pay fees, home pressure to leave school and bring in wages was very high. In 1935, at the age of 13, Alex Kerr came

home very pleased with himself. He had won a scholarship to stay on at school, take exams and get a good job. His father spoke to him. 'He told me to get a job and bring in wages. Within the month I was working at the post office.'

The giant of ignorance was tackled by the Education Act of 1944, which took effect in Scotland in 1945. It raised the school leaving age to 15 and all children were to get free secondary education.

Given the date of this legislation, clearly the Labour Government can take no credit for it, and it is another point in the argument that post-war social reform was not entirely the work of the new Labour government. In fact the wartime coalition began discussing education reform in 1941. The main idea at the foundations of educational reform was to be equality of opportunity and the creation of a system which would allow working-class children with ability to progress as far as they could without being restricted by the demands to pay expensive fees. However, the reality of the Education Act of 1944 was rather different from its original aims.

The credit for the education reform is given to RA Butler. He argued that the future of Britain's strength and wealth lay in scientific and technical training so technical education should be a priority. Butler's idea was to create a three-level education system of technical, grammar and secondary modern schools. In Scotland the last two were usually called senior and junior secondary respectively. Butler's original idea was for each type of school to have equal status but very soon the grammar/senior secondary schools were seen as the 'best' while the creation of high-quality technical schools never took root. It is argued that the influence of church people and politicians who were themselves products of private schools killed the idea of respected technical schools.

The desire to create a fair and socially balanced education system retreated in the face of reality. Although Prime Minister Churchill had stated that 75% of places in the very selective public schools should be opened up to pupils chosen by local authorities this idea gradually faded. There was a small increase in the proportion of working-class boys at grammar school but the real benefits lay with the middle classes. Grammar school fees were abolished, and government spending on the grammar schools and senior secondaries raced ahead of the expenditure on junior secondary moderns.

There was also concern about the use of exams at an early age to categorise children. Then and now many people opposed the idea of deciding a child's future at 11 or 12.

All children sat an exam at 11 (called the 11 plus exam, or the 'Qualy' in Scotland which was short for the qualification exam), the results of which decided the type of secondary school a child went to. For those who passed the exam the system worked well. They went to senior secondary schools and were expected to stay on at school after 15, go to university or get jobs in management and the professions.

However, those children who failed the exam went to a junior secondary and were expected to leave school at 15 and go into unskilled jobs. By failing the 11 plus, thousands of children were trapped in a world of low expectations and inferior education.

Butler had never intended such harsh decisions to be made about children in his original proposals but the reality of the education reforms became increasingly criticised – so much so that by the mid 1960s new thinking was moving state schools towards the comprehensive model, although that too has its critics.

What was done to improve housing?

In 1945 most of Britain's cities still had slum areas and overcrowding was still a serious problem, made worse by bomb damage during the war. After the two-night Clydebank blitz of 1941, for example, only seven houses out of a total stock of 12,000 remained intact. Cities across Britain suffered and as peace broke out a huge rebuilding programme was needed. Labour's manifesto recognised the need.

> "
> *Labour's pledge is firm and direct – it will proceed with a housing programme with the maximum practical speed until every family in this island has a good standard of accommodation.*

The government aimed to build 200,000 houses each year but economic conditions were not helpful – raw materials were in short supply and expensive. Nevertheless the government was successful. Although only 55,400 new houses were completed in 1946, by 1948 over 280,000 were built, way above the government's target. Many were council houses for rent and of those many were 'factory-made houses' – 'prefabs' for short – which were quickly assembled on site. Even in 1951 Labour still averaged well over 200,000 houses a year. Cities became encircled with council owned housing estates providing new, quality homes for those people moving from the inner cities. These homes were in many ways better than the overcrowded tenements left behind. On the plus side, the houses had separate kitchens, bedrooms and a living room. There was gas and electric power, hot and cold water, indoor toilets in a bathroom and most houses in the 1950s were two stories high, usually with gardens front and back. The down side was summed up by Alex Kerr, who moved from central Edinburgh to a council estate on the south side in the early 1950s.

> " I was far from my work, my friends and the town. I had to walk two miles to the nearest bus stop. The tar was still wet on the roads, there were cows in the fields behind us and when I came home from work there was just the tele, my wife and son. No pubs, no cinemas, not even shops at first. A chip van came round on Friday night. But all the neighbours were in it together. We soon made new friends.

Overall, the new council estates were a saviour for people living in crowded tenements in the centres of Scotland's cities. Not least among the advantages was the council's role as a major landlord which protected people from unfair exploitation by private landlords. In the 1950s council rent was one third of that in the private sector.

Unfortunately, nobody had foreseen the huge demand for housing after the war. The increase in marriages, the rapid increase in the birth-rate and the reluctance of families to continue living as extended families in cramped conditions all combined to swallow up houses as fast as they were built. Newspaper stories of families 'squatting' in disused army camps while they waited for housing, as at Duddingston in Edinburgh, all added to the impression that Labour had failed in their promise. In spite of Labour's undoubted achievement, given the difficult economic situation, there was still a serious housing shortage in 1951 and long waiting lists for council housing.

As part of the vision of a new Britain, and also to provide space for the increase in house building, a New Towns Act of 1946 gave the government the power to decide where new towns should be built and to set up development corporations to carry out the projects.

The aim was to create towns that were healthy and pleasant to live in as well as being geared to the needs of the townspeople, unlike the random, uncontrolled growth of Britain's 19th-century industrial cities. In Scotland, East Kilbride and Glenrothes are examples of post-war new towns with Livingston reflecting the vision of the New Towns Act although not growing until the 1960s. Altogether fourteen New Towns were established before the end of the Labour government in 1951.

Jobs for all?

The traditional view of post-war employment levels is that all governments from 1945 until the 1970s were committed to a policy of full employment, which means that everyone who wants a job can get one. In 1944 a White Paper (government proposals for discussion) seemed to accept the need to aim for full employment, and the Labour Manifesto of 1945 made its policy clear while at the same time raising doubts about the commitment of the other parties to achieving the goal of full employment.

> All parties pay lip service to the idea of jobs for all. Where agreement ceases is in the degree of control of private industry that is necessary to achieve the desired end. Our opponents say, 'Full employment. Yes! If we can get it without interfering too much with private industry.' We say, 'Full employment in any case, and if we need to keep a firm public hand on industry in order to get jobs for all, very well. No more dole queues, in order to let the Bosses of Big Business remain kings in their own castles.' The price of so-called 'economic freedom' for the few is too high if it is bought at the cost of idleness and misery for millions. There must be no depressed areas in the New Britain.

One answer to the problem of unemployment was nationalisation, which had its roots in Labour's socialist beliefs and was adopted as party policy after the First World War. In theory, nationalisation meant that the government would take over major industries and run them for the benefit of the country rather than the private owners. Profits would be used by the government rather than filling the pockets of private owners and in this way Labour believed they could control and manage the economy more effectively and maintain full employment.

However, revisionist historians now take a different view of Labour's policy and wonder just how responsible the government was for maintaining the goal of 'jobs for all'. When the Labour government began in 1945 there was a private expectation that unemployment levels would level out at about 8%. That was still a high number of people out of work but to the government's surprise unemployment levels tumbled to 'full employment' levels. What caused this? Quite simply, the boom in private investment and building after 1945 was a main reason. The need to recover and rebuild after the war soaked up workers and Labour took the credit.

So how successful was the Labour Government of 1945–1951?

Labour did try to deliver its manifesto promises despite serious problems right from the beginning. Victory in the Second World War bankrupted Britain and critics have pointed out that Britain was therefore in no position to launch a welfare programme. They argue that the government should have directed resources towards industrial reconstruction first to strengthen Britain's economy. Correlli Barnett, in *The Audit of War* (1986), argued that Labour's first priority should have been the re-equipping of industry and the development of technical education. Even Labour's own 1945 manifesto recognised the problem.

> *But great national programmes of education, health and social services are costly things. There is no good reason why Britain should not afford such programmes, but she will need full employment and the highest possible industrial efficiency in order to do so.*

Instead the Labour government focused on their attempts to build a fair society in Britain where help was available to all – often referred to as the 'New Jerusalem' of the welfare state. Barnett reminded readers that a central point of earlier social reform had been to increase national efficiency (remember the Liberal reforms?) yet Labour seemed to forget or ignore this point. He asked how far Labour's welfare reforms equipped the nation to compete against other nations.

Developing Barnett's ideas further, Professor Jose Harris, in *William Beveridge: A Biography* (1997), has shown that while most countries in western Europe increased their social spending after 1945, these other countries targeted their social spending on the labour force, with the aim of increasing industrial efficiency. In Britain spending was more generous towards the old, the sick and the poor, which had no direct economic benefit.

However it would be wrong to criticise Beveridge and the Labour administration between 1945 and 1951 for what they did not do. In the words of Sir Keith Berrill, a senior Treasury official, 'We had won the War and we voted ourselves a nice peace.'

Some critics have argued that the government was either doing too much for the people – leading towards the modern cliché of 'a nanny state'. On the other hand other writers have claimed not enough was done and the Beveridge Report was a lost opportunity to build a better Britain.

But these critics miss the point. The Beveridge Report provided a beacon of hope to war-weary people who wanted to believe that post-war Britain would be a land worth fighting for, and Labour's reforms went a long way to create a post-war Britain based on ideas of fairness and help for all who needed it. The living standards of the poor were raised and people looked forward to a time of increasing opportunity and prosperity. In the 1950s Conservative Prime Minister Macmillan told the British people they had 'never had it so good'. The prosperity and feel-good factor of the 50s had its roots in the improvements and reforms put into practice by Labour. By 1951 the Labour government had achieved a transformation of British society in a way that improved the lives of millions of people, male and female, young and old. For the first time the financial uncertainties of unemployment and serious illness were banished by the welfare state, and a start was made in providing decent housing and education for everyone.

Activity ▐▐▐▶

This activity is similar to the one outlined in the democracy and the franchise section when you were provided with a partly-completed spider/spoke diagram which illustrated the main themes in the section and also the detailed attacked to each theme. This time you must complete the whole diagram yourself.

Draw a spider diagram around the central question 'How did Labour tackle the social problems facing Britain between 1945 and 1951?'

- Around your central question draw five boxes. Each box should contain **one** of Beveridge's five giants.

- From each of the boxes draw at least three more legs, each one leading to a particular Labour reform which tried to tackle the social problem in the box.

- Draw a fourth leading from each of the giant reforms to include a brief assessment comment on Labour's success for failure.

Do that for all five of the giants. When you have finished you have the information needed to describe and assess what Labour did about each of the social problems identified by Beveridge.

Exam essays 📄

Other essay types in this section could be:

1 How successfully did the Labour government deal with the social problems facing Britain at the end of World War Two?

2 To what extent did the Labour government of 1945–1951 defeat the giant problems identified in the Beveridge Report?

7 The rise of political nationalism in Scotland 1880s–1979

Introduction

Between the 1880s and the outbreak of the Second World War in 1939 changing attitudes towards the union between Scotland and England sowed the seeds for what became known as political nationalism. In the 1880s most Scots thought of themselves as British. Scotland was controlled from London. By the 1930s the London-based government had made changes which granted some power to departments with responsibility for Scottish affairs based in Edinburgh. However, these changes were not enough for some Scots, who were arguing a case for separation from England and independence for Scotland.

Although the Scottish National Party was formed in the 1930s it was not until the 1960s that the SNP made a national political breakthrough. By the 1970s political nationalism allied itself to an emotional desire for 'freedom'. In 1979, by the end of this period studied in this course, the debate about Scotland's political identity had become such an important issue that the government held a referendum which asked the Scottish people directly how they felt about devolution. The vote went against the Nationalists but by the end of the century Scotland had its own parliament. The question of how far a desire for Scottish independence will continue to grow remains uncertain.

From the 1880s until World War One

In the 1880s most Scots were happy to be part of Britain and its empire. Many Scots did well by migrating to England or working abroad in the British Empire. One of Victorian Scotland's most famous Scots – Sir Walter Scott – declared that any political change would 'destroy and undermine until nothing of what makes Scotland Scotland shall remain.'

Being part of Britain offered Scots many opportunities. At this time Glasgow became the second city of the Empire. Scotland was part of the world's leading industrial and military superpower – Great Britain. However, there was a growing feeling that Scotland should have more MPs to represent Scottish interests. In 1880, Scotland had only 65 MPs out of 658. If MPs had been allocated on the same basis of population as in

England, Scotland would have had 90. Either way, Scottish socialists argued there was little chance of a Scottish working-class voice being heard since all Scots MPs were wealthy middle- or upper-class men.

By 1880 there was increasing pressure for Scotland to have more control over its own affairs. In Westminster, Scottish affairs tended to be rushed through with Scottish MPs urged to reach compromises quickly so as not to slow up the 'real' business of parliament. However, there was also a feeling that Scotland was definitely not 'North Britain' and that Scottish affairs should be looked after from a base in Scotland rather than in London. Consequently, in 1885 the Scottish Office was created. But its heart was at Dover House in London, with only a tiny presence in Edinburgh. Nevertheless it was a recognition that Scottish affairs were different from England's and required a separate administration. But even so, separate did not mean equal. A Scotch Education Department had been created in 1872 but the whole department was a single room, with the sign SCOTLAND on the door. The 'Scottish Room' was within the much larger Department of Education for England and Wales.

In 1892 the Scottish Secretary, who was in charge of the Scottish Office, was finally given a place in the Cabinet, the heart of political policy making in the government. But in the words of Michael Lynch, 'the Secretary's work was largely ceremonial and an ability to stir up apathy was one of the main talents it demanded.'

To the critics of a union which seemed to leave Scotland run merely as a department of England, the changes introduced around the 1880s were not enough.

In 1886 a Scottish Home Rule Association was formed. They argued for a Scottish parliament to look after Scottish affairs, but working within the UK political system – rather similar to the situation now. 'Home Rulers' did not campaign for independence. A more focused organisation associated with Home Rule was the 'Young Scots'. It argued that Scotland needed effective social reform immediately to solve problems of poverty, and only home rule could deliver that.

Source 7.1

Queen Victoria established her holiday home in Balmoral. The link between the royal family and Scotland was important in maintaining the strength of the Union.

Nevertheless, voices raised against the union were few in the years before the First World War and in the flush of patriotic togetherness which flooded over Britain from August 1914, the Scottish Home Rule Bill was abandoned by parliament. Power was still in the hands of London-based central government and despite pressure for changes in the way Scotland was governed, most Scots were happy to remain part of Great Britain.

Between the wars

Between the First and Second World Wars Scottish politics was pulled in two directions. While the British government tried to strengthen Scotland's position within the Union there were important developments in the attempts by some Scots to break the Union.

The 1930s also brought significant changes in public attitudes towards the Union. The inter-war years were times of high unemployment and poverty and there were some Scots who believed that the Union with England was no longer helping Scotland. Scots no longer saw England and the empire as being able to provide resources and leadership to overcome the economic and social problems affecting Scotland. Migration to England or the empire no longer promised a brighter future and Scotland was no longer the workshop of the empire. During the inter-war period, large-scale unemployment increased in traditional heavy industries such as ship building, textiles and coal mining. Central government was blamed for doing very little. Little attention was paid to the argument that it was tax income from the relatively prosperous south of England that helped pay for unemployment benefit and other government help programmes operated in Scotland.

Source 7.2

This tramcar was decorated to celebrate the end of the First World War. The Union Flag is prominent but no Scottish Saltire. The patriotism of war ended, for a time, hopes for Home Rule.

Attempts to strengthen the Union

Although the Labour Party's 1918 election manifesto promised to fight for 'The Self-Determination of the Scottish People' and 'The Complete Restoration of the Land of Scotland to the Scottish People', just how mainstream were such proposals? Even the Labour Party's commitment to

Home Rule faded after the collapse of the short-lived Labour government of 1924. In the 1920s all three major parties actively supported the Union.

The big parties were, however, well aware of the growing nationalist tendency in Scotland through the 1920s and had taken some steps to make Scots feel more 'involved' or recognised by the London government. In 1926, the Scottish Secretary became the Secretary of State for Scotland, the first man in the job being Sir John Gilmour. As part of the Cabinet, the Secretary of State was at the heart of UK government and Gilmour's strategy tied Scotland even tighter to the union. He staffed the Scottish Office, still based in London, with career civil servants whose aim was to serve the government of the day rather than promote Scottish interests. In another development, the Scottish Office was later moved away from London and relocated in St Andrew's House, Edinburgh. These new arrangements seemed to be a positive move which showed the importance that the British government placed on Scottish affairs. Another more cynical interpretation was that the move north was designed to strengthen links within the union just a few years after the founding of the Scottish National Party – a party whose intention was to break the Union.

Source 7.3

The first Secretary of State for Scotland was Sir John Gilmour. His strategy tied Scotland even tighter to the union.

The roots of the Scottish National Party

The Scottish National Party's origins can be traced back to a number of organisations which grew up in the 1920s. Pressure groups such as the Scottish Home Rule Association had tried and failed twice to get their aims translated into law.

At the same time there was a division between the old style Home Rulers who had their roots in the later Victorian period and the more radical nationalists whose purpose was to resist the erosion of Scottish culture and Scottish identity by the spread of 'Englishness' in all aspects of life. Artists, writers and poets, such as Hugh MacDiarmid, styled themselves as a 'Scottish Literary Renaissance' and took pride in their attacks on those who, in their view, had sold out to England. In the words of Michael Lynch, 'the atmosphere of nationalist politics (in the 1920s) was dynamic, vituperative, portentous and endlessly garrulous.' In other words active, argumentative and doom-laden!

Despite those divisions, the National Party of Scotland was founded in May 1928, described by Lynch as 'a glittering coalition of irreconcilable talents.' Its chairman and secretary, Roland Muirhead and John MacCormick, had grown up politically in the Independent Labour Party. In contrast, more artistic talents such as Hugh MacDiarmid were included within a party whose aim seemed to be a bit of a fudge in keeping with the mixed characters in the party – 'independence within the British group of nations'.

Perhaps that fudge was a reason for electoral failure. MacCormick and Muirhead received only 3,000 votes in the 1929 General Election, less than 5% of the vote in each constituency. In 1931 things were no better. The most successful candidate only polled 14% of the vote.

Source 7.4

Writers and poets such as Hugh MacDiarmid styled themselves as a 'Scottish Literary Renaissance' and took pride in their attacks on those who, in their view, had sold out to England.

By the early 1930s political groups supporting some form of home rule were split between two main groups, each with different views on the political direction of Scotland. The more right-wing Scottish Party faced the more left-wing National Party. After a mutually damaging by-election campaign in East Fife in early 1933, it was clear the existence of such apparently similar parties would simply result in continuing election failures. The result was a joining together of the two groups to form the Scottish National Party on April 7th, 1934 (the party only became known by its initials SNP in the 1960s). The merger of the two Scottish parties was simply due to practical needs in the face of political reality. There was certainly a need for a unified voice for Scottish nationalist hopes but the new Scottish National Party had very little direct political influence in the 1930s. For most Scots in the 1930s, poverty and unemployment were more serious issues than Home Rule, for which the Scottish National Party could offer no quick fix.

The Effect of World War Two

The outbreak of World War Two also caused some problems for the SNP. Government propaganda created a feeling of unity against Nazism and many films made by the government's Crown Film Unit showed Scots,

Source 7.5

Patriotism and propaganda once again made the prospect of breaking the union unthinkable. This cartoon from the end of the war in 1945 shows the archetypal Scottish laddie – Wullie – waving his Union Flag. Kilts can be seen but no Saltires!

English and Welsh fighting and laughing together, enduring war's hardships. In such an atmosphere breaking up the UK was an irrelevance, and unthinkable, for the duration of the war.

Arthur Donaldson, later the SNP Chairman in the 1960s, was imprisoned along with several other nationalists for his anti-war pacifist beliefs and in 1942 the party split over its attitude towards the war. John MacCormick, a core leader of the party left, took many supporters with him, and set up the Scottish Union, which later became the Scottish Convention.

On the other hand discontent with the government did grow as the war dragged on and in some areas of Scotland support for the SNP rose. In the Argyll by-election of 1940 Scottish National Party candidates won 37% of the vote and at Kirkcaldy in 1944 the party won 42% of the vote. Finally, at Motherwell in April 1945 the party won its first parliamentary seat, held by Dr Robert McIntyre. However, McIntyre's success was short lived and he lost his seat at the general election three months later as voters turned to promises of a brighter future under Labour. The Scottish National Party had no more election victories for another 20 years.

The post-war years

Throughout the 1950s political nationalism made little progress, although a speech given by war time Prime Minister Winston Churchill in the Usher Hall, Edinburgh in 1950 had raised some hopes. Churchill offered fresh 'guarantees of national security and internal independence', and an examination of 'the whole situation between Scotland and England'. He also offered a second representative in the Cabinet to protect Scotland's interests. Was this a new beginning for Scottish politics or a cynical

attempt to undermine Labour support in Scotland, win some support from nationalist voters and counter the emotional attraction of MacCormick's Scottish Convention? Either way Labour won the subsequent election and even when the Conservatives became the government throughout most of the 1950s the 'Scottish angle' in British politics was conveniently ignored.

The Scottish Convention

When John MacCormick left the SNP he went on to form the Scottish Union, soon renamed the Scottish Convention. Its aim was to draw together people from all walks of life and it operated as an effective pressure group, producing a Scottish Covenant (a written agreement) which demanded a Scottish parliament within the framework of the United Kingdom. The Covenant petition had 400,000 signatures within three months of its start and gathered over two million signatures between 1949 and 1950. This suggested there was large support in Scotland for the idea of 'devolution' or a form of home rule without seeking complete separation. However, the Covenant failed to become an electoral force and without an effective political voice the Labour government at the time ignored it. Publicity stunts such as replacing Union Flags on public buildings with Saltires and removing the Stone of Destiny from Westminster Abbey and smuggling it back to Scotland were dismissed as the work of eccentrics. Without clout at the ballot box it seemed that supporting some form of Scottish separateness was a lost cause.

For most Scots in the 1950s life was improving. Unemployment was low and housing, health and living standards generally were better than ever before. The discontent which had seen the SNP prosper on a protest vote in the war years had evaporated. The SNP got less than 1% of the vote at elections in 1955. For the twenty years after 1945 Scotland's voters divided more or less equally between the Labour and Conservative parties. The new Conservative government of 1951 forgot Churchill's promises of 1950. The Labour Party, which had supported Home Rule in the1940s, rejected it in the 1950s. The SNP

Source 7.6

John MacCormick was a founder member of the National Party of Scotland, who joined but later left the Scottish National Party and is best remembered for the Scottish Union, soon renamed the Scottish Convention.

THE GLASGOW UNIVERSITY MAGAZINE

JANUARY, 1951

John M. MacDonald, LL.D.
Rector

failed to fight any by-elections between 1952 and 1960, its membership stuck around 2000 and in the 1950s it seemed to be an irrelevance in Scottish politics.

But in the 1960s the political situation in Scotland changed again. The new Labour government needed its Scottish MPs to maintain its authority. To 'keep Scotland sweet' the government, fronted in Scotland by Secretary of State Willie Ross, made all of Scotland, apart from Edinburgh, a development area. As such, Scotland could expect government grants and incentives to help economic growth. Livingston and Irvine became new towns in 1966 and 1969 respectively while a new university was built at Stirling and older campuses were renovated and born again at Strathclyde, Heriot-Watt in Edinburgh, and Dundee.

Why did the SNP recover in 1970s?

In the late 1960s economic difficulties hit Britain. Public discontent with the government grew in Scotland and in the Hamilton by-election of November 1967 Winnie Ewing won the seat for the SNP, overturning the previous Labour majority of 16,000. In 1973, Labour suffered another crushing defeat at Govan when Margo MacDonald of the SNP became 'the blonde bombshell' of Scottish politics. By the early 1974 the SNP gained almost 40% of votes cast and had 11 MPs in parliament.

A common argument is that the SNP did better in times when Scots were unhappy with the British government and wanted to protest, and to an extent this is true. Scotland's traditional industries continued to decline and unemployment started to rise. At the same time oil and natural gas were discovered in the North Sea and in 1972 the SNP launched the effective 'It's Scotland's oil' campaign. Another SNP slogan, 'England Expects... Scotland's Oil',

Source 7.8

In 1967 Labour lost a majority of 16,000 when Winnie Ewing won the Hamilton by-election for the SNP. Not all of Scotland had been 'kept sweet'!

Source 7.7

By the late 1960s the SNP was increasing in popularity and votes.

Source 7.9

Oil Tankers at Sullom Voe Shetland – in 1972 the SNP claimed 'It's Scotland's oil'; their slogan captured the public imagination at a time when oil prices were rising fast. Was there a chance of real wealth for an independent Scotland?

seemed to suggest that England seemed to be getting richer by allowing Scotland to become poorer. The discovery of 'black gold' at a time when oil prices were rising fast seemed to offer the promise of economic wealth either for an independent Scotland or shared wealth within the Union.

Suddenly the oil industry was camped in Scotland. Shipyards which had been in decline started to make oil rigs and supply vessels and Shetland experienced a boom as Sullom Voe was developed as a major oil terminal in the later 70s and 80s.

How important were changing ideas about Scottish identity in the 1970s?

In the 1880s most Scots seemed happy to see themselves as British and even in the 1950s school text books would regularly use the word 'England' instead of Britain and few people objected. By the 1970s how far was the rise of a modern, assertive Scottish identity the result of a definite political campaign for independence by the SNP? Or did the SNP ride a wave of nationalism that had its roots elsewhere? Teenagers wore the white and blue SNP badge almost as a fashion accessory. Songs ranging from the Corries' 'Flower of Scotland', to assorted World Cup anthems such as 'Ally's Army' in 1978 reflected a youthful and emotional nationalism. Pop bands such as The Bay City Rollers made a feature of their 'tartan image', while punks such as The Skids from Dunfermline and the Rezillos from Edinburgh made it cool to be Scottish. England as a synonym for Britain was no longer acceptable in Scotland.

Devolution or not?

The rising national consciousness of Scots had political consequences in London. Both Labour and Conservative parties began to speak of some form of devolution – in other words giving Scots some control over their

The rise of political nationalism in Scotland 1880s–1979

In the 1970s the Bay City Rollers were just one example of a growing public indentification with Scottishness as opposed to Britishness which the SNP hoped to transform into electoral success.

In November 1977 separate bills for Scotland and Wales were introduced and on 1 March 1979, Scotland seemed to have voted in favour of devolution. But the result was confusing. 63% of the electorate voted and they split into 32.9% 'Yes' and 30.8% 'No'. Although it seemed as if the yes vote had won, there was a catch. Just before the referendum vote a new rule had been made in parliament. It stated that for Scotland to win devolution, 40% of the **whole** Scottish electorate would have to say yes.

When the results were declared, the 'yes' vote was still a long way short of the target. Supporters of devolution called it a 'fix' and the

own affairs but still retaining effective control from London. Both main parties were worried about the attraction of the SNP, whose support peaked in 1977 at 36% of the electorate.

The introduction of devolution legislation in the 1970s was largely the product of nationalist pressures on the Labour government, which needed to keep its support in Scotland to remain in power. Under pressure from the SNP, the Labour government agreed to propose a Scotland and Wales Bill in November 1976. This built on the Kilbrandon Report of 1974 which recommended the establishment of a Scottish parliament and supported the idea of devolution. However, the bill was rejected by parliament.

In 1979 hopes for a Scottish parliament were flying high, but were dashed when the devolution vote failed to gain the necessary majority.

SNP claimed that it simply proved England would never easily give up its control over Scotland.

The 1979 referendum was the closest Scotland had yet come to devolved power within the UK. But full Home Rule – or devolution – would not come another 20 years. The answer as to why devolution became a real possibility in the 1990s has never been fully or easily answered. Was it through pressure of the SNP? Was it a major change in the assertiveness of a definite Scottish identity? Was it the result of political deals in closed rooms? The only easy answer to the question why Scotland is now devolved is that Scots voted for it.

Activity

In this activity make up at least ten questions which you would use to test someone's understanding of the main issues and developments in the rise of political nationalism in Scotland 1880s–1979.

To construct good questions you must first understand the issues you are assessing and ensure your question is not vague, ambiguous and does focus attention on the key issue. One word answer questions such as 'who was…' or 'when was…' are not allowed!

Your questions should be mature, well presented and test real understanding. The purpose is to help learning, not to catch people out with really obscure or tricky questions.

When you have both completed ten questions, try them out on a partner. Can they answer your question? And can you answer your partner's question in exchange?

The ones to remember are the questions you did not know the answers to. They provide a guide to what you are less sure about.

Exam essays

Other essay types in this section could be:

1 To what extent can support for the SNP be described as reflecting the ups and downs of Scotland's economy?

2 The SNP is part of a long line of discontent with the union with England. Do you agree with this view of the rise of political nationalism in Scotland between the 1880s and 1979?

Changing Scottish society 1880s–1939: the impact of urbanisation on Scotland

Introduction

Urbanisation means the growth of towns and cities and was caused by the movement of people into the cities during and after the industrial revolution. By 1850, one Scot in five lived in one of the big four cities – Glasgow, Edinburgh, Dundee or Aberdeen. By 1900, it was one in every three.

Such rapid growth of cities had many consequences. Older patterns of living changed as people realised cities could offer anonymity and freedom from the constraints of small town life and the influence of the church. It is also possible to argue that urbanisation changed the way that Scots felt about themselves and their country. The focus of this chapter is on how urbanisation affected religion, education and leisure in Scotland between 1880 and 1939.

Urbanisation and change

As cities grew there was a need to manage and control the massive populations and this role was increasingly taken on by local authorities as the influence of churches declined. One example of that change was in education, which had to change to meet a demand not only for manual workers with basic literacy skills but also for white collar jobs and the professions.

The city population also had increasing leisure time, and with more money left over after the essentials were paid for the people looked for entertainment. For the wealthier sections of society the urban centres could be places of culture, prosperity and business but the middle classes regretted the loss of influence of the old traditional foundations of social order – especially the church. A rootless, more anonymous workforce who could lose themselves in cities felt free from the older traditions of local life. The Church of Scotland, commonly called 'the Kirk', was facing a serious challenge to its influence.

Source 8.1

This view of the east end of Edinburgh illustrates the urban experience for thousands of ordinary Scots in the late 19th and early 20th century, crowded together in smoky, dark blocks of tenements divided only by the deep valleys of the roads.

What impact did urbanisation have on the Scottish churches?

The Kirk and society

As early as the 1840s, Thomas Chalmers, a significant figure in church politics at the time, declared the large towns contained 'a profligate, profane and heathen population' who were a disgrace to Christian civilisation. It is also argued that it was concern about the 'heathen masses' in the urban slums that led to the church sending missionaries into the dark centres of towns and the wave of church building which took place in Scotland's inner cities in the later 19th century.

In the cities the Kirk became identified with the values of the middle classes and the skilled working-class. Even the tradition of wearing 'Sunday best' clothes to church might have created a social division, with those too poor to have changes of clothes feeling excluded. By the end of the 19th century attendance in Church of Scotland services varied, with the Kirk being seen by many working-class people as the provider of services to hatch, match and dispatch – more formally, baptisms, marriages and funerals. Kirks became filled by the serious-minded families of skilled artisans and the middle-class members of congregations who shared in the Victorian values of hard work and self help.

In some cities church missionaries even went into the slum areas to preach the gospel to those who no longer saw the church as relevant to their needs. Those missionaries also promoted temperance – the avoidance of sin and temptation, in particular a refusal to drink alcohol, which was considered a social evil which led to poverty and illness. The temperance movement was supported by all churches and associated organisations, one of the most famous being the Band of Hope.

Source 8.2

The middle classes moved out of the inner cities to find a better quality of life in the suburbs and they still exterted much influence on Scottish religion, education and leisure activities.

Millions of children belonged to Band of Hope groups and by 1900 there were over 10,000 weekly Band of Hope meetings across the country, all of which encouraged members to 'sign the pledge' – a promise not to drink alcohol. The Band of Hope was also fun. Magic Lantern shows (like modern PowerPoint presentations) were a great novelty, while in summer children were taken on day trips to the countryside or the seaside. One member wrote in 1932:

Source 8.3

The Band of Hope was a hugely popular temperence organisation around 1900. This group from St. Mungo's church, Leith would have 'signed the pledge'.

> *The Temperance friends catered for the people's enjoyment by starting excursions to the seaside... for many who had never seen the sea. Special trains were run and filled at various stations, with as many as 2,000 people at a time.*

Those who support the argument that the Kirk was losing its influence by the end of the 19th century point to reports such as the Church of Scotland's Life and Work Committee which reported in 1874 that less than 200,000 of its almost 700,000 members had been present at communion in that year and by the end of the 19th century the Church of Scotland was openly referring to 'the lapsed masses' – those who, for whatever reason, had drifted away from the teachings, and the authority, of the Church of Scotland. This view of declining church influence continuing into the 20th century was summed up by AC Cheyne in The Transforming of the Kirk (1983)

> *Long-established traditions (such as) churchgoing and Sabbath observance continued to give ground before the onward march of technological progress and social change. Improvement in communications – faster trains, ... the electric tram, the motor bus, and above all the private car... – hastened the decline of rural society. It also undermined the hold of custom by introducing people to a new and vastly different way of life and enabling them to escape more easily from that which they no longer desired to follow.*

On the other hand, more recent historians such as Callum Brown, in *Religion and Society in Scotland since 1707* (1997) and David Hempton, in *Religion and Political Culture* (1996), have argued that church membership did not collapse and religious values continued to influence the Scottish way of life. Church membership in Scotland doubled between 1830 and 1914, peaked at an all-time high in 1905 and 'even non-churchgoers sent their children to Sunday school, dressed up on Sundays, sang hymns, respected "practical Christian" virtues, and derived comfort from religion in times of suffering or disaster.' Even in 1956 levels of Church membership were only marginally lower than in 1905.

The Catholic Church in urban Scotland

After the huge immigration boom from Ireland in the 1830s and 1840s the Catholic community in Scotland became more settled and by the 1880s the Catholic Church was well established in central Scotland. The church not only provided help and a sense of belonging to those who had arrived in Scotland poor and homeless, but also a secure shelter against anti-Catholic prejudice and discrimination.

By 1880 Scotland's cities, such as Dundee, were well served by newly-built Catholic churches and newly-trained clergy as described by WM Walker.

> *In the early 1860s the physical evidence of the Irish catholic presence in Dundee consisted of two splendid churches and three schools. Within a little more than 10 years the number of churches and schools was doubled.*
>
> *Juteopolis: Dundee and its textile workers 1885–1923.*

In the later 19th century there were criticisms of the Catholic Church creating a protective wall around its people, with its clergy warning of the dangers of mixing with Protestants and thereby losing their own distinct identity. The wicked word of the time was 'assimilation', meaning Catholic Scots mixing with non-Catholics and drifting away from a 'pure' Catholic identity. But was the Catholic Church doing anything more than other churches were in the changing world of urbanised Scotland?

The Catholic Church could argue that it was their superior organisation and commitment which led to their various social and self-help organisations operating under the umbrella of the church. For example The St Vincent de Paul Society and the League of the Cross, created to help the poor and combat the evils of alcohol, shared many of the same Victorian values of hard work, saving and temperance as the Protestant church.

In some ways the Catholic Church was becoming stronger than the Protestant churches after 1880. In the words of Tom Devine:

> *While some of the Protestant churches were arguably losing touch with the urban poor at this time, the Catholic clergy were forging ever closer contacts with them. A new social Catholicism was emerging which created almost an alternative community in Scotland for the Irish immigrants and their descendants.*
>
> *Tom Devine, The Scottish Nation.*

Partly in an attempt to prevent assimilation through intermarriage, the Catholic church developed a network of social activities where Catholic young men and women could socialise. Even Celtic FC has its roots in deliberate attempts to keep young Catholics together in their leisure time. In fact many of the football teams of central Scotland reflect the need to provide a strong Catholic identity in a changing and sometimes threatening world. Apart from Celtic, Hibernian in Edinburgh (Hibernia the old name for Ireland) and Dundee United (originally Dundee Hibernian) are examples of a need for identity and a sense of belonging. On the other hand, the existence of Protestant-based teams with anti-Catholic roots might suggest the Catholic community had a need for such identity and belonging in the face of opposition.

Source 8.4

The combination of Irish flag and Celtic FCs crest is a reminder of the Catholic Irish contribution to the Scottish way of life.

Sectarianism was still common in the workplace where Protestants feared and resented Catholics, who they saw as a threat to jobs and homes. The Orange Lodge, which became established in Scotland in the 19th century, was a voice and visible demonstration against Catholicism in Scotland. Conflict between the two groups was common as shown in this 1938 description of a Saturday evening in Glasgow.

> *I was looking out from a window of a coffee house in Argyle Street about seven o'clock of a Saturday evening. I heard flute music then I saw a procession. It was a company of Orangemen in full uniform... They had just gone by when a new music came to us and a new procession appeared. They were Hibernians. 'Orangemen and Hibernians!' we said to ourselves, 'What will happen if they meet?' Some resourceful and sporting policemen diverted both parties into a side street and left them to fight it out. Such incidents give Glasgow afternoons and evenings their distinctive flavour!*
>
> *Sketches for a portrait of Glasgow in Scotland, 1938.*

By 1914 the old tensions seemed to be fading and in the First World War Catholics and Protestants fought side-by-side, with six Catholic soldiers winning Victoria Crosses for bravery. However, after the war, as economic depression struck Scotland, old tensions began to re-emerge. Catholic families who had lived in central Scotland for several generations once again found themselves labelled as 'alien Irish' threatening Scottish culture and jobs.

In March 1929, the Glasgow Herald quoted a letter sent on behalf of the Scottish Protestant Churches to the Secretary of State for Scotland.

Changing Scottish society 1880s–1939:
the impact of urbanisation on Scotland

> *There is even a danger to the continued existence of Scottish nationality and civilisation. We are convinced that a law abiding, thrifty and industrious race is being supplanted (weakened) by immigrants. ... The Irish race in Scotland keep largely to themselves, and their habits are such that our Scottish people do not readily mingle with them.*

By 1930 sectarianism revived as hard times and unemployment provided an opportunity for some politicians to feed on old, buried prejudices. Edinburgh, for example, witnessed anti-Catholic rioting provoked by John Cormack's Protestant Action, an organisation which blamed Scotland's economic problems on foreigners and immigrants – especially Irish Catholics living in Scotland. Cormack persuaded many people in Edinburgh that their problems were caused by the Catholic minority and spoke openly about the need to 'crush' and 'liquidate' the Catholic–Irish menace. His propaganda led to Catholics being excluded from employment, threatened in their homes, churches and schools and attacked on the streets.

One Edinburgh woman, now in her 80s, recalls how respectable employers openly refused Catholics work.

> *There were certain shops, they'd ask you what school you went to, and if you said Saint something or other they'd just say, 'Sorry, it's been taken.' In other words, they wanted to find out what religion you were.*

Cormack did not cause anti-Catholic feeling in Edinburgh. He simply breathed life into old hatreds. In the 1930s the Church of Scotland gave its support to a campaign to stop immigration into Scotland of 'inferior' and 'alien races' (mainly Irish Catholics) which lasted until 1938, while the Scotsman newspaper complained that Catholic Archbishop James MacDonald was overreacting after he protested to the government about the policies of Protestant Action.

However in 1939 such sectarian divisions were forgotten when World War Two began and the tensions which had revived such tribal differences were buried under the common need to fight Nazism.

Educating the People

In the late 19th century Scots took pride in claiming that the Scottish education system was among the best in the world.

It was true that Scotland had five universities when England had only two and there was a lasting belief that pupils from ordinary backgrounds – the

'lad o' pairts' – could rise to find success. A schools inspector's report in 1872 explained how a boy in England from an ordinary background would find it impossible to get to university but, 'In Scotland useful ability, prudence (being sensible) and hard work are the only requisites (requirements).' The Scottish education system therefore appeared *meritocratic*, which means people could achieve success through their own efforts. A report from the Educational Institute of Scotland in 1903 expressed the belief in Scotland's educational system – 'The ideal of free opportunity for all... is one vitally active in the Scottish people.'

But was it truly a meritocracy? Or did changes brought in the wake of urbanisation create a myth, a nostalgia for the good old days when all children were taught in local parish schools and all were successful? In other words did urbanisation make education worse, better or just different?

The function of schools

As Scotland changed and cities grew questions were raised about the purpose of education in an industrial, urbanised society. What should be taught? How should it be taught? Why should it be taught? And should schools also fill a social and even religious purpose? As a church minister reported:

> " *The young are so constantly encompassed (surrounded) by endless temptations and means of indulgence, and at the same time parents themselves are generally so unable to discipline their children, that the only likelihood of having them reared in Christian knowledge is to provide it in the daily schools of instruction.*

Urbanisation and industrialisation increased demand for mastery of the 3Rs of reading, writing and arithmetic (nowadays called functional literacy) in the creation of future white-collar workers such as civil servants, office workers and business people. It was also argued that an educated work force was needed since governments of the time felt Britain's position in the world was slipping. Urbanisation also led to the rapid expansion of cities with huge numbers of poorer working class people who, in earlier times, might have been feared as an unruly mob. That group, combined with migrants from the country, needed to learn the importance of time keeping, rule following and strong discipline. For all these problems and difficulties, schools seemed to be the answer.

The Scottish Education Act of 1872 said that all children aged between 5 and 13 had to go to school, but parents had to pay a small amount of money for each child. Although some poor families complained about the fees and still sent their children out to work, the school boards inspected the work done in each school and kept a check on pupils' attendance. An entry in the School Log of St Mungo's school, Balerno for December 1898

Source 8.5

Attendance officers enforcing attendance at schools were part of everyday life – even for Oor Wullie in this 1937 cartoon.

stated, 'Some of the elder scholars are still away working. The Birrels and the McArdles are the most irregular although the attendance officer receives their names every week.'

Parents were not allowed to use poverty as an excuse when they kept their children away from school and inspectors enforced the law with the result that attendance rates at school became more regular. An elderly woman in Leith remembered:

> What they used tae cry (call) the School Board came to the door for ma brother Harry because he was off the school. Ma mother told them that she couldnae afford to buy him a pair o' shoes. She was waiting on ma dad's boat comin in.

Complaints about fees ended in 1890 when education became free in state elementary schools for 5 to 14 year olds. Fees were still charged for secondary school and for most children, especially those from poor backgrounds, their education in school ended at the age of 14.

By 1908 school boards were also trying to deal with health issues by providing medical inspection of pupils and, in some areas, school meals. Teachers were expected to check heads of pupils for lice (or 'nits'). Jean Fairbairn of Leith remembered:

> I tell ye what wis rife when I wis at the school, ring worm, and that wis infectious. It wis mostly among boys though, and they got their hair cut. They had tae get it scalped. And they were taken away from the school. The nurse came round and she examined ear, nose, and throat, and yer teeth.

Teachers also organised help for children still walking barefoot to school. Miss Elizabeth Cockburn, a teacher in Leith wrote:

> One of the sad things I remember was the police used to send boxes of boots to the school. They were the coarsest, most dreadful boots. I remember yet having to fit them out with the boots saying 'See if they'll fit you,' If they hadn't got these they would've gone about in their bare feet, bare cold feet. There was terrible poverty.

For the sons and daughters of the middle-class, there was a wide choice of schools. In the urban centres there was a boom in fee-paying schools which provided a quality education for the new elite. In Edinburgh, George Heriot's School, the Merchant Company schools such as George Watson's and Mary Erskine's and the chateau-like Fettes College soaked up the children of the upper-middle classes. In Glasgow a similar service was provided by Kelvinside Academy and Hutchesons' Grammar. Even in St Andrews a socially-exclusive boarding school education for middle-class girls was provided at St Leonard's.

Source 8.6

The chateau-like Fettes College soaked up the children of the upper-middle classes.

For the lower-middle class of office workers, shopkeepers and even schoolteachers who wanted something better for their children some schools were created, partly funded by the state but 'topped up' by a modest fee paid by parents.

Changing Scottish society 1880s–1939: the impact of urbanisation on Scotland

The SED provided grants for 'Higher Grade Schools' and the Edinburgh Evening Dispatch of 25 August 1904 described such schools:

> ### EDINBURGH NEW HIGHER GRADE SCHOOLS
>
> *The opening of the school session this year will mark the beginning of a new era. This is the opening of the two Higher Grade schools – Boroughmuir for the South and Broughton for the North side of the city.*
>
> *Clear and regular instruction will also be given in science, literature and commerce and the organisation will enable pupils to receive a thorough general education and the best training for Leaving Certificates and University entrance examinations.*
>
> *As Primary and Secondary between them will provide accommodation for 2200, Broughton will be one of the largest, if not the largest, in Scotland.*
>
> Adapted from The Edinburgh Evening Dispatch, 25 August 1904.

Secondary education was, however, not for all as one Edinburgh man remembers.

> *I won a scholarship to the Royal High. But in those days my father, who was just a sheet metal worker, didn't have a good wage. The scholarship was £100 but my mother and father thought it over. The teaching was free but you had to buy all the sports gear and clothes and books. You had to buy everything except the education. So they actually turned it down.*

In 1918 the Education Act allowed local authority education committees to take over the running of schools, including Roman Catholic schools which were now funded by the state.

Until 1918, Catholic schools had received no financial help from the government and instead had to rely mainly on voluntary contributions, which put huge pressure on a mainly poor Catholic population who raised funds through weekly offerings, collections, fairs, concerts and small-scale social functions. For some time the SED had been concerned that the Catholic community would suffer from the difficulties of funding schools adequate to their needs and that Catholic children might be doomed to continue in low-skilled, low-paid jobs.

In exchange for agreeing to the state taking over the administration and financing of their schools, only teachers acceptable to the Catholic Church 'in regard to religious faith and character' were employed, and religious instruction was to continue unrestricted. Priests were also allowed access to all Catholic schools.

The 1918 Act angered the Church of Scotland and other Protestant groups. They complained about 'Rome on the Rates', in other words government money spent on Catholics who, they said, should join in with non-Catholic schools if they wanted to benefit from 'free' education. At the time, rates were a kind of local taxation paid for by all people, hence the resentment by some Protestants of the money being spent on supporting Catholics.

On the plus side, the 1918 Act was very important in encouraging Catholic assimilation into Scottish society and for improving the opportunities for Catholic children. A good education was seen as a passport for social improvement by those who had moved into the towns and wanted a better life for their children and Tom Devine sums up the advantages of the 1918 Act.

> *Without it, the Scoto-Irish may have been unable to grasp the educational opportunities of the twentieth century and as a result be condemned to the enduring status of an underprivileged and alienated minority.*

Historians argue about the purpose of education in early-20th century Scotland. Was it to educate all or only to create an educated minority who would fill the administration and managerial jobs of the urbanised society?

HHM Paterson and TC Smout argue that the education system failed the Scottish people because it was mainly targeted at the needs of the middle classes. The system did little to improve the social mobility of the working classes. Indeed, Paterson claims the schools system for the bulk of the population in Scotland was 'mass schooling so as to recruit talent to the leader class whilst, at the same time, placating (keeping quiet) and controlling the many'. Smout agrees, arguing that education was, 'a matter of low social priority once the perceived needs of the middle classes had been attended to.' Despite the intention of the Education Act of 1918, Tom Devine observed:

> *The vast majority of working-class girls and boys left school as soon as they could to enter the factory, pit, farm, of office or domestic service. But this was caused fundamentally by the economic pressures on ordinary families and their social expectations rather than the nature of the educational system itself.*

In 1914 only 4% of Scotland's children completed secondary education and only 2% went on to university level. By 1939 the figures were much the same.

Leisure and popular culture

Between the 1880s and 1939 Scotland's urban population had more money to spend and greater choice about how to spend their leisure time than ever before. Real wages – what wages could really buy – increased and with shorter working hours and the increase in holidays workers had the opportunity to spend their money. In many trades working hours had fallen from 60 hours each week to 48 hours. A half-day holiday on Saturday was already common in cities by 1880 and by 1890 a week-long, but unpaid, summer holiday was not unusual. By 1914, 'trades fortnight' meant 14 days rest for some industrial workers.

Between 1880 and 1939, urbanisation produced a huge potential audience for mass entertainment, for example in the cinema or the football stadiums. On the other hand the churches still retained their influence as a focus for popular leisure activities, even for those people who never attended church services.

'Healthy' activities such as walking, cricket, gardening, bowling and, above all, golf were also very popular. Cycling clubs also became hugely popular with people rushing out of the urban centres at weekends although it had some problems.

> "
> *In our cycle club we all wore black shirts. One day near Roslin we were stopped and beaten up by some people who thought we were Nazi supporters out for some trouble. I didnae go back next week. I couldnae afford a new wheel.*
>
> Mary McNeil, a teenager in the 1930s.

The influence of the churches

Despite the attractions of new entertainments, the churches remained the centre of much popular entertainment until the 1960s. Children went to youth clubs and Sunday Schools. Churches organised picnic outings to the seaside or countryside, dances and sports days. The Boys Brigade was hugely popular with teenage boys with over 35,000 members in 1939. They enjoyed the marches, the bugles and also the swimming and football leagues. But members of the Boy's Brigade also had to attend church. For girls, the Girls' Guildry and Girl Guides provided suitable leisure activities.

The temperance organisations linked to the churches also organised their own football leagues with over 70 teams playing in the Band of Hope Union Cup.

Leisure as social improvement

Local authorities, and the middle classes, believed in the old saying, 'the devil finds work for idle hands'. With increasing leisure time, what would the working classes do? The temptation of 'rough culture', defined as drinking alcohol, gambling, football and 'street life' generally was obvious. What could be done to counter those attractions and in some way 'improve' the character and morality of the urban masses?

In Scotland's cities libraries, art galleries and public halls were built to bring culture to the masses. In Edinburgh, the Royal Scottish Museum in Chambers Street was built in 1904, in Aberdeen the Art Gallery opened in 1885, and in Dundee a museum and art gallery opened in the 1870s. These were all attempts at widening the horizons of the urban population. In response to concerns that the masses would not flock to places offering 'high-brow' culture, the People's Palace on Glasgow Green offered a combination of culture and entertainment to those who might not have thought of the two things going together! In its first year 770,000 people went to its attractions.

To improve the health of the people local authorities built public parks and municipal baths, sometimes with a swimming pool attached such as Infirmary Street Baths in Edinburgh. As the name suggests, people from tenements could go to those places simply for a bath – otherwise no such opportunity for washing would have existed. Public parks offered the chance to walk in fresher air for people who would maybe never see the country or have a garden. In the parks, games such as putting were played but 'no ball game' signs were hated by boys looking for a rougher game of football.

At weekends, concerts could be listened to around newly-built bandstands. The Caird Hall in Dundee, the Usher Hall and McEwan Hall in Edinburgh and the Cowdray Hall in Aberdeen were also opened, financed by rich local businessmen, and provided a focus for more 'high-brow' cultural experiences.

Source 8.7

In its first year 770,000 people went to the People's Palace on Glasgow Green which offered a combination of culture and entertainment.

The Demon Drink

Pubs became the stronghold of the semi- or unskilled working man. They provided warmth, light and the friendship of pals, away from the demands of children, wives and the reminder of poverty in overcrowded tenements. While some pubs remained 'spit and sawdust boozers', new brightly-decorated pubs, with large gas lamps and opaque glass windows giving a hint of the bright life inside, became common in the cities tempting drinkers inside with an atmosphere of glamour and leisure in contrast to the dark cold streets of urban Scotland.

The churches were heavily involved in combating the appeal of 'pub culture' and temperance organisation such as the Rechabites, the Band of Hope and the Independent Order of Good Templars asked their members to take 'the pledge'. After the Great War some local authorities even went completely 'dry' which meant that no alcohol was sold. Most of these areas were 'wet' again by the 1930s, but pubs still closed at 10pm and didn't open on Sundays until well into the 1970s.

By the 1930s consumption of alcohol had fallen and it seemed that Scots had found other leisure activities to distract them from 'pub life'. Certainly by the 1930s less whisky was being drunk, but that was more likely the result of higher taxation pushing up the price. By the 1930s 'pub culture' was in decline as a result of the growing popularity of alternative activities and entertainments on which surplus incomes could now be spent. As a popular song of the time went

> *Aye he's fitba' crazy he's gone clean daft,*
>
> *Since he started playing fitba' his heid has gone right saft,*
>
> *For he willnae drink a whisky and he's never in the pub,*
>
> *Since oor Jock became a member o' that terrible fitba' club.*

Fitba' crazy

Although cricket, rugby union, rowing and bowling had all become popular among the skilled working classes, nothing could challenge the attraction of football. The first Scottish club, Queen's Park, was founded in 1867 and the Scottish Football League was born in Holton's Hotel, Glasgow, on 20th March 1890. Ten clubs joined including famous names of today such as Celtic, Rangers and Heart of Midlothian as well as some which have since declined, such as Cambuslang and Cowlairs.

The spread of trams and railways had a huge influence on the development of football leagues. With half-day Saturday holidays professional football became big business. Within cities electric trams carried huge numbers of spectators to and from the football grounds while the spreading network of railway lines allowed national leagues to be created with fans travelling between cities all in the space of a Saturday afternoon and evening. Before 1914 it was common at big games for over 70,000 to attend and in 1937 a crowd of 149,515 watched Scotland play England. At the time it was a world record.

Football could be played almost anywhere and cost almost nothing. At first the teams which were established in the cities were made up of workmates or memberships of other groups, such as Queens Park which grew out of the YMCA. For talented players football provided an escape from a life of work for low pay and long hours. For the fans football provided an identity, a sense of belonging to a 'tribe' and hours of escapism following the ups and downs of 'oor team'.

Source 8.8

For talented players football provided an escape from a life of industry work for low pay and long hours.

Holiday time

The development of leisure at this time is closely linked to developments in transport. Railways took city people into the countryside and day excursions to the southern highlands, especially the Trossachs, became popular. The development of a steamboat and paddle steamers, especially on the Clyde, allowed the urban population in the west of Scotland to go 'doon the watter' to the Clyde seaside resorts of Rothesay, Dunoon or just to cruise around the Kyles of Bute. Edinburgh's crowds could relax on Portobello beach or travel to North Berwick or Dunbar and risk freezing in the open-air swimming pools. By the end of the 1930s a weeks holiday with pay had become normal and during the summer trades week or fair holiday trains could take holiday makers further, even to Blackpool or Scarborough.

8

Source 8.9

The Marine Hotel, North Berwick. Middle-class holiday makers from Edinburgh were attracted to the seaside attractions and the golf courses of East Lothian. Railways provided the transport.

Street life

While football could be justified by those who wanted to 'improve' society in that it provided exercise in the fresh air and encouraged a competitive spirit, 'street life' activities, sometimes called 'rough culture', and new forms of mass entertainment caused the middle classes and the churches to shake their heads in disapproval. Dancing, music halls and later cinemas and especially gambling were all considered unsuitable activities.

For many urban Scots gambling involved dog racing. In the days before betting shops and television, horse racing was a relatively unknown sport in urban Scotland but greyhound racing, which started in Britain in 1926, was very popular. It provided a chance to gamble legally.

Dog races were held in cities during the evening, and they offered legal, on-track betting such as at Powderhall in Edinburgh. However, such activities were frowned on. Gambling was believed to be a trap in which the poor stayed poor by risking what little money they had. But anti-gambling campaigners missed the point that gambling was also a source of excitement and offered at least the possibility of escape from poverty. Local authorities tried to stop gambling by passing local laws which stopped bookies taking bets and the police were given the job of stopping illegal gambling. However, the increasing popularity of 'respectable' and legal gambling such as the football pools made attempts to stop other means of gambling difficult to enforce.

Entertainment for the masses

Commercial, large-scale entertainment meant music halls, theatres, circuses, and, by the early 20th century, cinemas.

Music halls, which provided variety shows with dancers, comedians, jugglers and singers were hugely popular with the working classes. Stars emerged who became internationally famous such as Harry Lauder with his stereotyped tartanised caricature of a 'Bonnie Hieland Laddie'. But with the coming of cinemas urban mass entertainment changed.

By the 1930s, Edinburgh had over 50 separate cinema buildings (not just mutliplex screens) and Glasgow had double that number. Even small villages such as Crail and Pittenweem in Fife had a cinema each. The standards of the cinemas varied. At Edinburgh's New Victoria, opened in 1930, audiences sat in a cinema designed to be similar to an ancient Greek amphitheatre with a star-studded ceiling representing a Mediterranean sky. At the Salon Cinema, opened in 1913, 'they used to squirt disinfectant over you. It wasn't a nice picture house. It was a flea pit'.

Cinemas were hugely popular. In 1937 a survey of 8,000 West Lothian schoolchildren found that 36% attended the cinema once a week and a quarter more often. Many were cheap to get into. The Grand in Edinburgh accepted jam jars as payment for a while. The cinema could reclaim the deposit on the glass jars later from local shops. They provided escapist entertainment and by the 1920s film stars such as Clara Bow and Rudolf Valentino influenced the fashions of Scottish youth. By 1939 the common complaint that Scottish culture had been Anglicised had changed into protests about spreading 'Americanisation'. When American film star

Source 8.10

This queue of children was for the Picturedome, an early cinema in Edinburgh's Easter Road. Going to 'the pictures' was a popular leisure activity for most Scots, sometimes as often as three times a week.

Changing Scottish society 1880s–1939: the impact of urbanisation on Scotland

Clark Gable took off his shirt to reveal a bare chest in the movie *It Happened One Night* (1934) the sale of men's vests in Scotland fell!

Churches complained about the dangers of young people spending hours together in the darkness of the cinemas but for most Scots the cinemas brought a wider world into their local area for the first time.

Variety theatres and music halls became considerably less popular in the 1920s and 30s as a result of competition from cinemas. But another form of mass entertainment – dancing – was also on the rise. Glasgow was described as 'Dancin' daft' in the 1930s with 159 registered dance halls in 1934. The Saturday night dance became the high point of the week for thousands of young Scots from all social backgrounds. Sometimes the shock of the new was not always good as Alexe McKenzie remembered. 'We got all dressed up and went to the dancing at Fountainbridge. I like the slow dances where the lads held me tightly but one night I saw lice crawling out of one boy's hair onto his shoulder.'

Source 8.11

Scottish cities became 'Dancin' crazy' in the 1920s and 30s. Before the spread of dance halls, church functions had been the likeliest place to find one's future husband or wife. This 1950s pictures shows 'chattin' up' in progress!

The overall effect on Scottish culture

In the 1880s most rural Scots had strong individual dialects and made their own, usually communal, entertainment. Neighbours who could play a musical instrument such as an accordion, or tell good stories, were welcome visitors. There was no opportunity to hear any voice or sound from outside their own area unless they met a visitor or travelled themselves.

By 1939 it was harder to define what was Scottish culture. Although radios were still not cheap they marked the beginning of the end of

communal leisure time with a uniquely Scottish identity. In their houses, Scots found a new source of entertainment which spoke to them in 'proper' English from the only radio station available – the BBC.

In the theatres and music halls they laughed as Harry Lauder, dressed in kilt, 'bunnet' and carrying a curly walking stick made gentle fun of old fashioned versions of Scottish identity. In the cinemas, Scots were exposed to the values and fashions of the Hollywood studio dream factories. In dance halls Scots danced to the latest American jazz and big band 'swing' music.

It has been argued that the last strongholds of urban Scottish identity were the pubs, the football terraces and the dog tracks. Elsewhere influences from outside Scotland were changing how Scots spoke, thought, dressed and behaved. In the more isolated rural areas, still not connected to electricity even by 1939, an older Scotland lived on until the arrival of television and the widespread use of the motor car.

Source 8.12

By the 1930s motor transport was providing different leisure opportunities and changing the way of life of most Scots.

Urbanisation had widened the horizons of thousands of Scots and exposed them to new influences. In 1939 Scotland was still influenced by the values of the church and in many ways still retained old customs and habits. The huge social changes which were to come in the 1950s and 60s were still unthought of. But on the other hand urban Scotland in 1939 was very different from that of 1880.

Activity

To be successful in this section you must be aware how urbanisation affected religion, leisure and education. This activity will help you to select and organise relevant information.

1 Write the heading 'Urban change in Scotland 1880–1939'

2 Beneath your heading divide a page into three columns. Title one column Religion, the second Leisure and the final column Education.

3 In each column list at least eight facts for each topic you would include in an essay on change (more facts would be good)

4 Shade each column a different light colour (avoid heavy marker pens)

5 Draw another chart entitled Changes between 1880 and 1939.

6 Once again make three columns entitled Religion, Leisure and Education.

7 Give yourself space to write a few lines under each heading.

8 In each column write two sentences briefly identifying the main themes you would develop in an essay on urban change in Scotland between 1880 and 1939.

You have now done a different version of the spoke diagram activity elsewhere in the book. You have selected and organised information and also planned out your main themes you would indicate in an essay introduction. Your columns of facts provide you with the detail you would include in an essay to develop your main ideas.

Exam essays

Other essay types in this section could be:

1 To what extent did the process of urbanisation affect religion, education and leisure in Scotland between the 1880s and 1939?

2 Education may have changed but religion and leisure remained unaffected by changes in urban Scotland between the 1880s and 1939. Do you agree?

Index

Index

Index